MW01256778

OLD-FASHIONED ECONOMICAL COOKING

OLD-FASHIONED ECONOMICAL COOKING

Healthy Culinary Ideas on a Budget

By
Winifred S. Gibbs
Dietitian and Teacher of Cooking for the New York Association for Improving the Condition of the Poor.

Foreword by Leanne Brown

Racehorse Publishing

First published in 1912 by The New York Book Company

First Racehorse Publishing Edition 2017

Racehorse Publishing books may be purchased in bulk at special discounts for sales promotion, corporate gifts, fund-raising, or educational purposes. Special editions can also be created to specifications. For details, contact the Special Sales Department, Skyhorse Publishing, 307 West 36th Street, 11th Floor, New York, NY 10018 or info@skyhorsepublishing.com.

Racehorse Publishing™ is a pending trademark of Skyhorse Publishing, Inc.®, a Delaware corporation.

Visit our website at www.skyhorsepublishing.com.

10 9 8 7 6 5 4 3 2 1

Library of Congress Cataloging-in-Publication Data is available on file.

Cover design by Lori Wendin
Cover artwork: iStockphoto

Print ISBN: 978-1-944686-56-7
Ebook ISBN: 978-1-944686-58-1

Printed in China

Table of Contents

Foreword 7
Preface 9

PART I
INTRODUCTION

Food Values 13
How to Plan Meals 15
How to Buy Economically 17
How to Tell the Age of an Egg 22
Kitchen Equipment 23
Arranging an Attractive Table 26
Dangers of the Kitchen 27

PART I
RECIPES AND MENUS

I. Recipes and How to Use Them 29
II. Beverages 33
III. Bread, Biscuits, Rolls, Muffins, Etc. 37
IV. Batters 41
V. Cake 43
VI. Canning and Preserving 50
VII. Casserole Cooking 52
VIII. Cereals 54
IX. Chafing Dish Cookery 56
X. Cheese 58
XI. Confections 61
XII. Decorations 63
XIII. Eggs 65
XIV. Fish 68
XV. Frying 74
XVI. Fruits 76
XVII. Frozen Desserts 79
XVIII. Macaroni and Other Italian Pastas 81
XIX. Meat—Game—Poultry 83

XX. Milk 90
XXI. Nuts 91
XXII. Pies 93
XXIII. Puddings and Sauces 95
XXIV. Relishes 100
XXV. Salads and Dressings 102
XXVI. Sandwiches 106
XXVII. Soups 108
XXVIII. Special Cooking 114
XIX. Vegetables 117
Bibliography 120
Menus for All Seasons 121

PART III
MISCELLANEOUS

Government Bulletins 133
Government Charts
Breads, Etc. 134
Cereals 135
Milk and Cream 136
Eggs and Cheese 137
Meats 138
Butter, Lard and Oils 139
Fish 140
Vegetables 141
Fruits 142
Sweets 143
How to Read the Gas Meter 144
A Comparative Study of Fuels for the Housewife 145
Managing a Gas Range 148
Glossary 149
Birth Month Gems, Flowers, etc. 152
Wedding Anniversaries 152
Index to Recipes 153
Table of Abbreviations 158
Table of Weights and Measures 158
Time Table for Cooking 159
Household Hints 160

FOREWORD

You've picked up *Old-Fashioned Economical Cooking*, a cookbook from 1912 by a woman named Winifred Gibbs. You're curious; what was life like one hundred years ago? How did the stoves work? More importantly, were the pancakes as good?

Usually when we study history we study the major events: the invention of the first vaccines, women's suffrage, school desegregation. *Old-Fashioned Economical Cooking* dispenses recipes and advice for daily domestic life. It tells the story of everyday—the soil in which major historical events grow. It's reality television, not *CNN*; Pinterest tutorials, not the *New York Times*.

Ms. Gibbs's goal is for her readers to get the most for their food dollar. Beyond filling up on a bunch of potatoes, they should be nourished with *healthy* food. But what does that mean?

The best healthy eating advice has not changed in one hundred years. Mrs. Gibbs states plainly that a "mixed diet is suited to all persons." Currently, Dr. Oz exhorts his viewers to eat all the colors of the rainbow and Michael Pollan decrees we "eat food, not too much, mostly plants." What has changed is how we consume, develop, and publicize information. The fast pace of news cycles privileges new information, making it seem like health advice is always in flux. It makes it seem like we never know if eggs are good for us. But the truth is simple—eggs are good for you, just don't eat too many—it's practicing healthy eating that is hard.

Mrs. Gibbs isn't here to tell you it will be easy. In her world, healthy food is relative. If you sit at a desk all day, you need a salad. If you are doing physical labor, meat and potatoes are the healthier, economical choice. Family taste and means are part of the equation. And rather than dispensing blanket advice, she advises her readers to become experts, learning how cake batter should "feel" and how bread "sounds." Become a master; don't just follow directions. Respect food as the primary source of energy for your body.

The problem for the modern reader is not with Mrs. Gibb's advice itself, but her assumption of who implements it; the homemaker and only the homemaker. For Mrs. Gibbs the homemaker was just like her: a woman. The homemaker role was not chosen, but expected. The obligation to cook, and to cook with a smile on your face, is what changes cooking from a creative, important endeavor with clear positive outcomes—full tummies and a delicious experience—to a soul-sucking onerous chore. I hope I don't need to explain why women should not be expected to take this on. Let's simply roll our eyes and look forward.

If we can ignore Ms. Gibbs's outmoded notions of who is doing the work, replace the word "housewife" with "every member of the household," "she" with "they," then we can see with fresh eyes the egalitarian vision of *Old-Fashioned Economical Cooking*. Regardless of how much money the world has afforded you, you deserve good food. This is the core of Ms. Gibbs's work, as true today as it will be in one hundred more years. I could not agree more.

—Leanne Brown, 2017

THIS little book aims to be both instructive and suggestive. The principles of right feeding, economy, and cooking are set forth, with a variety of recipes and menus, and it is hoped that the general public will be interested in these important subjects.

The book is planned for housekeepers who wish to begin simply, but the importance of attractive food and service is insisted upon as bearing directly on the health of the family.

The recipes are planned for two persons, with the idea that they may be quite easily adapted to a larger number.

These rules have all been tested, and many of them are family favorites.

Thanks are due to my assistant, Helen E. Smith, for efficient help in the preparation of this book, and to Mrs. Mary Hinman Abel and Miss Minnie M. Smith, for permission to use recipes from their writings. Also for quotations made from Miss Anna Barrows' "Rules for Cooking Fish."

W. S. G.

PART I.—INTRODUCTION

FOOD VALUES

EVERYONE wishes to get the best possible results from time and effort put into daily work.

It is equally important to make each penny expended for food bring in as much strength as possible.

A practical knowledge of food values fits the housekeeper to really " feed " her family—that is, to see that tired muscles are built up, overwrought nerves calmed, and all forms of bodily weakness overcome.

The busy housewife need not plunge deeply into chemistry, but she should learn the few great classes of food, and what each does for the building up of the body.

We may temporarily overcome " hunger " by eating a quantity of bulky food such as potatoes, when really our bodies have not been fed properly at all.

What Every Housewife Should Remember

We depend on food to build up the strength used in daily life.

If we let stimulants take the place of food, we use up strength faster than we can make it, as stimulants give only a false strength.

Food is necessary for warmth.

A mixed diet is best suited to all persons. This means:

Bread and butter. Cereals. Rice or potatoes. Vegetables and fruits. Meat, eggs, or milk. Sweets.

Children's stomachs have not "grown up," so to speak, and we must not expect them to do the same work—that is, digest the same kind of food as adults.

The constitution of everyone is largely influenced by the kind of food eaten during childhood.

In the treatment of disease, most modern physicians consider that proper diet is more important than medicine.

Classes of Food

For convenience, foods are divided as follows:

1. Proteids—strength-giving foods, to give muscular endurance.

Meat. Milk. Eggs.

2. Fats, to give flesh and heat.

Fat of meat. Butter. Cream. Oils. Oily parts of nuts.

3. Sugars and starchy food, to give endurance and flesh.

Sugar. Molasses. Breads. Cereals.

4. Vegetables and fruits, to harden the bones, to purify the blood and to keep the blood in good order.

5. Water. This is food as well as drink, for it helps to keep the body from wasting away, and it also cleanses the entire system.

We need equal parts of strength foods and fat, and about three times as much of the bulky, starchy foods, such as cereals and bread.

To sum up, a "well-fed" person is one whose food contains materials for keeping him warm, for building muscle, for making flesh, for keeping the blood right, for making the bones firm, and, in short, for keeping the body in perfect condition.

The selection of foods to meet these conditions is discussed in the following chapter.

HOW TO PLAN MEALS

The old idea that a person should eat what he "craves" is not a safe one to follow, since he may crave food that is actually harmful, or, at least, that which is useless for nourishing the body.

To plan meals wisely, it is necessary to think of several things:

First. The ages, occupations, and general health of the different members of the family.

Second. The proper combinations of foods to fill these needs.

Third. The season of the year.

Fourth. The cost of food.

Foods Suited to Various Ages

Bottle-fed infants need very carefully prepared milk (see Chapter 28).

Foods for children from one to two years are discussed on pages 114-115. Above all, the mother should remember that the truest kindness sometimes lies in not considering the whims or fancied dislikes of children, but in giving food that is known to be the right food, and in teaching self-control and obedience.

Much suffering in after life may be avoided by this training, and the child will grow into a man or woman with a good fund of resistance to bad dietetic habits; even the deadly alcoholism may be more easily fought, if there is an inherited tendency.

Foods Allowed Child Two to Four Years

Eggs—soft-boiled. Stale bread and butter. Baked potato. Broths, cooled and skimmed. Zwieback. Orange juice. Boiled fish.

Milk. Beef juice. Boiled rice. Junket. Prune juice. One or two tablespoonfuls of mashed and strained peas, onions, or carrots.

Child Four to Eight Years

To the above there may be added:

Slightly larger servings of vegetables. Broiled steak or chop. Custards. Cream of vegetable soups (see page 112). Simple puddings. Very ripe scraped bananas. Baked bananas. Cocoa.

Child Eight Years and Upward

Practically the same as above, except that servings are larger.

Foods Forbidden All Children

Tea and coffee. Pastry. Rich puddings. All fried food. Pickles. Fancy sauces for meat or fish. Alcoholic drinks.

How Occupation Influences Diet Needs

Persons who sit at work must have light, easily digested food, and food that contains much nourishment in small space.

Those who are active may eat more "hearty," bulky food, especially if their work is in the open air.

General Health

If any member of the family is out of health, a physician should be consulted, and the diet prescribed followed very carefully, as the very life of the person may depend upon this care.

Proper Combination

Study the chapter on Food Values, and learn the kinds of food that best build up the body. For example, if the allowance of butter or other fat is small, increase the amount of starchy food. If very little meat is eaten, see that there are plenty of eggs, milk, etc.

Consult the list of foods making up the "mixed diet," page 14, and you will have a guide.

Remember that spicy, greasy, or heavy food is equally injurious for grown persons as for children, only that the former are not so easily made really ill as are children.

HOW TO BUY ECONOMICALLY

Buying economically is simply buying in such a way that every penny spent will return as much strength as possible.

Ten cents spent for rice will not give as much strength as ten cents spent for bread or oatmeal.

We know in a general way how much strength-giving food is needed, and the following table or diet list shows how various quantities of different foods, all making for the same amount of nourishment, vary in cost.

Food	*Amount*	*Cost*
Milk	7 pts.	$ .35
Round steak	1 lb.	.18–.20
Eggs	20	.80
Oysters	4 pts.	1.00

This table does not show the amounts of fat and starch in the different foods, but is given simply in an attempt to interest housekeepers in the subject of the cost of food. Anyone will see the advantage of knowing the relative cost of necessary food, as obtained in different foodstuffs, and will realize that it is folly to spend one dollar if the same strength-giving material may be had for fifty cents.

This is only the beginning of the subject, however, for it is the business of the housekeeper to see that the food purchased at fifty cents is adapted to the needs of her family in other ways, that it is in suitable form for the individual digestive peculiarities, etc.

It is literally true that we "live by what we digest," so that, at certain times, and for certain persons, oysters are the right and economical food to buy, even although we could get the same amount of strength from some other food at half the cost.

For the normal family, however, in their ordinary, daily living, it is worth while to study carefully how to make the less expensive food attractive, so that money may be saved for other needs and health-giving pleasures.

It is not the plan of this little book to do more than suggest lines of study.

How to Buy Milk

The only economical way to buy milk is to buy it from a reputable firm, and from one whose dairies, bottling plant, shipping depots, etc., are freely open to inspection. Otherwise, there is danger of disease. "Loose" milk is never safe.

Clean milk in clean bottles is really a cheap food, as it contains strength in a form quickly digested, and for the money spent, it gives a large proportion of nourishment.

One of the bulletins issued by the Department of Agriculture at Washington * shows that even skim milk is a good and economical food; the fat lost in the cream can be made up from other foods.

Luncheon of Bread and Milk

Bread	8 oz.	$ .04
Milk	1 pt.	.05
Total cost		$ .09

The above luncheon, this bulletin points out, gives one third the amount of strength needed for an entire day, and the same

* Farmers' Bulletin No. 74

amount of strength would cost more than double in the form of an ordinary restaurant luncheon of soup, meat, bread, and coffee.

The preparation of milk is discussed in another chapter, page 114.

How to Buy Meat

Expensive cuts of meat do not give as much strength as the cheaper cuts, and much money may be saved if care is taken to cook the meat so as to make it appetizing and digestible.

It should be remembered, however, that some of the cheap cuts contain much bone and waste, so that, in the end, they are not really cheap.

Table of Cuts of Meat

Very cheap meat.

Liver, .09–.10
Heart, .05–.07
Tripe, .07–.10
Oxtails, .10 each
Beef kidney, .12–.15
Beef brains, .10
Fresh beef trimmings, .06–.08
Calves' brains, .12–.15
Lamb kidneys, .03 each
Lamb tongues, .06–.08 each

Meat for stock.

Brisket, .06–.08
Neck, .10–.12
Shin, .08–.09
Shoulder, .07–.09
Mutton—neck, .08
Lamb—neck, .09

Meat for Braising, Boiling, and Stewing

Beef. *Boiling*—Round, .20–.22
Brisket, .09–.10
Stewing—Chuck, .12–.14
Shoulder, .10–.12

Veal. *Stewing*—Neck, .14–.15

Mutton. *Boiling*—Leg, .18–.19
Stewing—Neck, .08–.10

Lamb. *Stewing*—Breast, .10–.12
Neck, .08–.10

Steaks and Chops

Beef.

Skirt steak, .12–.15
Flank steak, .14
Round, .20–.22
Sirloin, .22–.23
Porterhouse, .24–.27

Chops

Veal, .15, .20, .23, .24

Mutton.
Shoulder, .15–.16 Loin, .20–.22

Meat for Pot Roast, Baking, etc.

Beef.
Shoulder, .12–.14 Chuck, .14–.15 Round, .20–.22

Mutton.
Shoulder, .09–.10 Breast, .08–.09 Neck, .08–.09

Lamb.
Breast, .10 Shoulder, .12 Neck, .10

Meat for Roasting

Expensive for small family.

Beef, .20–.40 Mutton, .16–.22 Pork, .18–.20

Note.—The above are New York prices.

How to Buy Staple Groceries

Whenever possible, such things as flour, sugar, potatoes, etc., should be bought in quantities, as they are always cheaper purchased in that way. If it is necessary, however, to buy in small quantities, through lack of storage space, we should ask for a fixed amount, as "three quarters of a pound" or "a quarter of a pound," but never "ten cents' worth."

The housekeeper should read the storekeeper's scale while he is weighing the food purchased, and then weigh it again on her own scales at home.

How to Buy Fruit and Vegetables

These should be neither under-ripe nor over-ripe.

If bought from pushcart vendors or at open stands, skins must be washed and removed.

Cuts of Meats

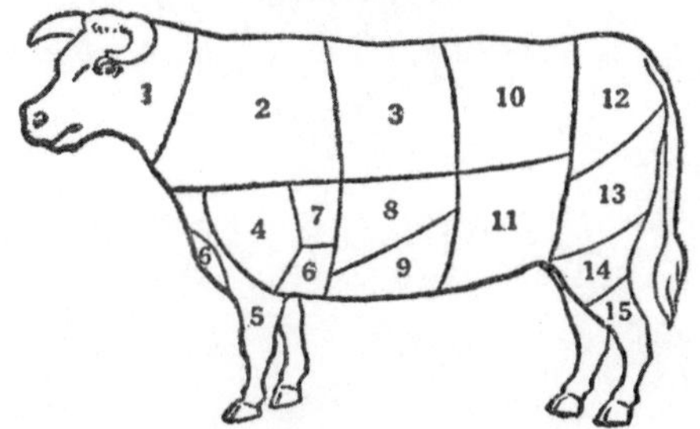

CUTS OF BEEF

1. Neck.
2. Chuck.
3. Ribs.
4. Shoulder.
5. Fore Shank.
6. Brisket.
7. Cross Ribs.
8. Plate.
9. Navel.
10. Loin.
11. Flank.
12. Rump.
13. Round.
14. Second cut Round.
15. Hind Shank.

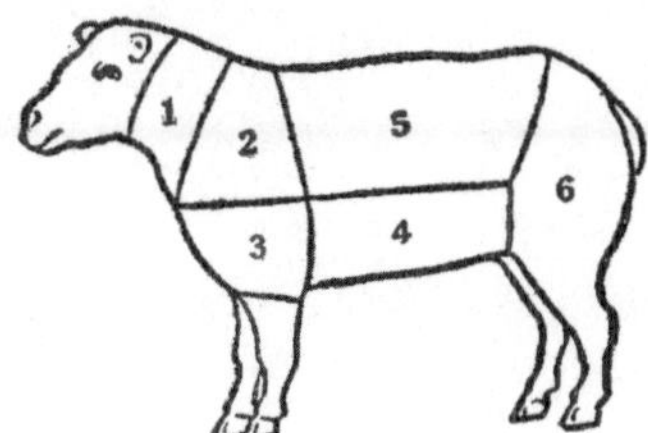

CUTS OF LAMB AND MUTTON

1. Neck.
2. Chuck.
3. Shoulder.
4. Flank.
5. Loin.
6. Leg.

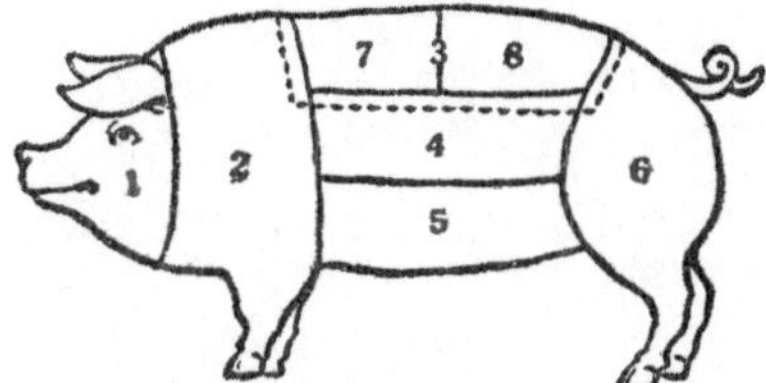

CUTS OF PORK

1. Head
2. Shoulder.
3. Back.
4. Middle Cut.
5. Belly.
6. Ham.
7. Ribs.
8. Loin.

How to Tell the Age of an Egg

Place the egg in a tumbler two thirds full of water and note the following:

If perfectly fresh the egg will rest at the bottom of the tumbler as shown in figure 1.

If not quite so fresh, say from two to four weeks old, the big end of the egg will rise higher than the small end.

If two, three or four months old the egg will take the position shown in figure 3.

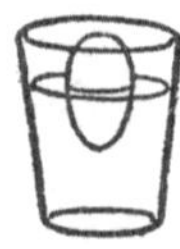

If older the egg will float upright, the larger end rising out of the water as shown.

The cause of this is due to evaporation within the shell. As the egg becomes older the water evaporates and the empty space at the thick end of the egg enlarges. The larger the empty space the more the egg will rise until in time it floats upright as shown, the larger end rising out of the water.

KITCHEN EQUIPMENT

Agate Ware

1 saucepan, ½ pt.	Soup kettle, 4 qts.	1 double boiler, qt.
1 saucepan, qt.	1 pudding pan	1 coffeepot
2 saucepans, pt.		

Tin Ware

1 biscuit pan	2 bread pans	1 measuring cup, ½ pt.
Flour sifter	Grater	1 funnel
1 wire broiler	1 wire toaster	2 milk pans
1 sugar sifter	1 salt sifter	1 dish pan
1 tea canister	1 coffee canister	1 small strainer
6 covers, different sizes	3 pie tins	1 large strainer
1 hand basin	1 tea kettle	

Wooden Ware

1 meat board	1 chopping bowl	1 small wooden spoon
1 vegetable brush	1 rolling-pin	1 large wooden spoon
1 scrub pail and brush	2 brooms	

Iron Ware

1 cast-iron frying pan	1 scale for groceries	3 Case knives
1 chopping knife	1 palette knife	3 forks (steel)
1 carving knife	1 can opener	3 tablespoons (plated)
3 teaspoons	1 Dover egg-beater	Scissors
Wire dish cloth	1 corkscrew	1 meat pan
1 meat chopper		

Glass Ware

6 Mason jars, qt.	6 Mason jars, pt.	1 lemon squeezer

Earthenware

1 casserole	6 custard cups	12-qt. mixing bowl
2 pt. bowls	1 teapot	2 stone jars for bread, etc.

Several small saucers and plates that will stand heat.

1 garbage pan	Chafing dish	Fireless cooker

Equipment

The above plan is for a family of two, and takes for granted that the housekeeper is willing to get along without some conveniences. It is a good plan to begin with the bare essentials and add utensils from time to time.

The question of labor-saving devices needs thought. Undoubtedly a large family can save time and strength by using some of the practical ones, but the young housekeeper will do very well if she has a good bread mixer and a fireless cooker.

Fireless Cookers

Very practical fireless cookers can be made at home, but small ones can be bought at low cost, and the housewife will

do well to add one to her kitchen, as much fuel and labor may thus be saved.

The principle involved is a simple one—that is, the holding of all heat and making this heat carry on the cooking.

Begin the cooking exactly as if it were to be carried on in the regular way—fifteen minutes for vegetables, thirty for stew or soup—and then place the covered kettle of food in the cooker without an instant's delay, cover tightly, and leave for twelve to fifteen hours, according to food.

It is well to remember that the cooker will simmer, but will not boil food. Anything that needs rapid boiling must be cooked on the stove, but tough meat and most vegetables may be cooked slowly.

Construction and Use of Home-made Fireless Cooker

MATERIALS NEEDED

Galvanized iron garbage can, "No. 2,"
Sawdust,
Two yards denim,
Covered agate pail, 2–4 qts.

Method

Place loose sawdust in bottom of can, so that when food kettle and top cushion are in place all space will be filled.

Fold denim lengthwise, make a long bag, about two inches deeper than food kettle, fill with sawdust, lay flat on table, spread sawdust evenly, and roll bag around food kettle, so that a smooth, firm nest is formed when bag is placed upright in can on top of sawdust. From remaining denim make a round bag (the material will have to be pieced for this), fill with sawdust.

Use of Cooker

Begin all cooking precisely as if it were to be carried on in the ordinary way. When food is at boiling heat, after having boiled the required length of time, place quickly in nest formed by long cushion, cover with round cushion, place galvanized cover over all, and let stand for required time.

The following is a table showing foods best adapted for preparation in the home-made cooker:

Article of Food	*Time on Stove*	*In Cooker*
Stew	30 m.	15 hrs.
Soup (meat)	30 "	12 "
Cereals	15 "	12 "
Legumes	30 "	15 "
Dried fruits	15 "	12 "
Pot roast	30 "	15 "
Vegetables	15 "	12 "

ARRANGING AN ATTRACTIVE TABLE

Food may be of the best quality and perfectly cooked, and if it is put on the table in a helterskelter way, or served on sticky dishes, it may fail to nourish properly those who eat it.

This is only another way of saying that digestion is easily influenced by small things.

On the other hand, if it is necessary to plan meals that are very inexpensive, the food will give more strength if great care is taken to make it attractive, since even the plainest food, wisely selected, will be digested quickly if it is attractively served.

Some rules for arranging a table attractively:

1. See that the table itself, even if it is of the plainest wood, is rubbed free from any stickiness or dust.

2. Economize on quality, if necessary, but have spotlessly clean tablecloths and table napkins.

3. Do not be unhappy if you cannot have expensive china and glass. An ample stock of pretty blue and white or even plain white china is better than one or two costly pieces and a general supply that is chipped or cracked. Wonderfully pretty china may be bought at very low cost.

4. Whenever possible, have a bit of green in the middle of the table. On country walks gather wild flowers or ferns for this. In the winter you may be able to have some berries or bright foliage, and it will add much to the pleasure of the table.

5. Housewives keeping house in a modest way do not need solid silver. A moderate supply of good plated ware will give perfect satisfaction, and if kept bright and shining will give another touch of attractiveness.

6. In whatever room the table is set, try to have it near a window, for a shaded dining table is very unsatisfactory.

7. A general rule that includes all the others is: No matter

how simple, let the table show absolute cleanliness and attention to detail, and this will give a result that can be attained in no other way. Members of the family will be influenced unconsciously, and all will enjoy it.

THE DANGERS OF THE KITCHEN

Care of Food

The chief danger of the kitchen is, to use a good old-fashioned word, dirt. Good housekeepers have always fought dirt instinctively, but we are coming more and more to realize just why it was such a menace to health.

Dirt gives a breeding place for the countless tiny living things that are in the air all about us. Many of these little bodies are harmless, some are really beneficial, but there are some that cause disease. It is very foolish to make ourselves miserable about these germs, but it is a good thing to think about them enough to make sure that we have no corners where they will grow. Cleanliness, light, and air will keep them out better than anything else.

Some Good Rules

1. Buy at stores where everything is kept clean.
2. Do not use raw fruit and vegetables that have been exposed to the air of the streets or to careless handling.
3. Boil drinking water if there is any reason to suspect its purity.
4. Keep all utensils, bread, pie, and cake tins, etc., scalded, dried, and aired.
5. Keep all parts of the ice box cleansed frequently with boiling water and soda.
6. In washing dishes, change the water frequently and rinse every dish in hot water after washing in hot suds.
7. Keep dish cloths and sink cloths scalded, sweet, and clean.

8. Do not allow pet dogs and cats in the kitchen.

9. Never allow insect pests to get headway. Cockroaches, water bugs, etc., may be driven out by care, but it is better not to let them get in. There is a phosphorescent paste on the market that is the best thing to use if these pests do show themselves.

10. Never leave soiled dishes or broken bits of food about the kitchen.

11. Fight the common house fly, as it may easily carry disease.

12. Remember that here, as in most other things, " an ounce of prevention is worth a pound of cure."

PART II

CHAPTER I

RECIPES AND HOW TO USE THEM

Principles of Cookery

MANY old-time cooks used very few rules, relying on what they called "judgment," and being quite scornful of rules. Modern domestic science women sometimes go to the other extreme and depend so entirely on rules that they do not exercise their reasoning powers.

A good plan is to be very exact, but to use this very "judgment" in adapting recipes.

No recipe can be written so as to exactly meet all conditions. Different grades of flour absorb varying amounts of moisture; cornstarch will vary in thickening qualities; flavoring extracts will vary in strength; sugar will not always have the same sweetening power.

Select recipes that have been tested, and if, in the working out, they need slight changes, learn how to do this intelligently.

A little practice will teach just how cake batter should "feel" on the spoon, just how bread "sounds" when it is baked, just the moment when boiled frosting is done, etc. The point is to train the eye and hand to work together, so that one need not depend on others, but will "know" oneself.

There are a few principles of cooking that form the foundation of all science. Each of the great classes of food spoken of on page 14 is governed by one or more of these principles.

Flavoring

Flavoring extracts should never be added until near the end of the cooking.

The Cooking of Meat, Milk and Eggs, or Strength Foods

Meat and egg-white are somewhat alike in structure, and heat affects them in very much the same way. Heat that is too intense hardens these foods, making them tough and indigestible. This applies to the heat used in boiling, and the rules for boiling eggs and meat insist on slow cooking or "simmering." In broiling or searing meat, heat is used to form a coating which keeps in the juice.

In making soup, meat is plunged in cold water to draw out the juice.

The point as to just what changes take place in the boiling of milk is still unsettled; but most physicians agree that the nutritive value of the milk is changed, and that unless there is danger of contamination by disease germs, it is better to use raw milk for infant feeding.

There is, of course, no objection to the cooking of milk in custards, puddings, etc.

The Cooking of Fats

Fats are used in cooking chiefly in frying, and the proper use of the term "frying" is not always understood.

Properly speaking, frying means dropping in a kettle of deep fat, and the common practice of browning food in an omelet pan is called sautéing.

The aim in cooking with fat is to see that it is hot enough to cook the food without soaking into it.

Fat is ready for cooked mixtures if it will brown a bit of bread while one counts forty, and for uncooked if it will brown the bit of bread while one counts sixty.

In sautéing, see that pan and fat are sizzling hot before the food goes in, otherwise the food will be greasy.

The Cooking of Starchy Food

The first necessity for this is rapidly boiling water, the second, long continued cooking. If these two rules are observed, cereals, potatoes, etc., will not be pasty and sticky.

The Cooking of Vegetables

Most vegetables contain some starch and a woody substance besides, and the above rule of beginning with boiling, not "hot," water holds good here, also, although the length of time required is not so great as that needed for cereals.

Thickening with Flour or Cornstarch

The two methods most commonly used to prevent flour or cornstarch from lumping are:

1. Rubbing to a smooth paste in cold water; then adding paste to boiling water, stirring constantly.

2. Blending with melted butter or fat; then adding boiling liquid to make a sauce.

White Sauce

This is used as a basis for "cream" soups, for creamed vegetables, meat, fish, eggs, etc., and in making croquettes.

The proportions for the three grades of thickness, as ordinarily used, are as follows:

Thin White Sauce

4 tablespoons fat (butter, oleomargarine or dripping).
3 tablespoons flour.
1/8 teaspoon salt.
Few grains pepper.
1 pint milk, hot but not boiling.

Medium White Sauce

4 tablespoons fat.
6 tablespoons flour.
1 pint milk.
Seasoning, as above.

Thick White Sauce

3 tablespoons fat.
2/3 cup flour.
1 pint milk.
Seasonings, as above.

Method

Melt fat—rub in flour, stir to keep smooth, pour on milk gradually, blending carefully; season; cook five minutes.

Use of Steam

The use of the double boiler or of an improvised one (p. 28) is necessary in cooking all starchy food.

In cooking of eggs in custard, by standing cup or pan containing mixture in larger pan of hot water, the egg is kept from separating or "curdling."

Cooking Processes

Boiling—in boiling water.
Stewing—"Simmering."
Broiling—Over direct heat.
Roasting—Cooking in the oven.
Baking—Cooking in the oven.
Frying—Cooking in deep fat.
Sautéing—Cooking in small quantity of fat.
Braising—Combined stewing and baking.
Fricasséeing—Sautéing and stewing.

CHAPTER II

BEVERAGES

BEVERAGES are important, as they give the necessary fluid to the diet, and their wise selection and careful preparation add much to the attractiveness and healthfulness of the daily meals.

Cold Beverages

Water

Few persons drink enough water. At least one quart a day should be taken, besides what is found in food. Part of this water may be taken in the form of beverages, but nearly everyone is the better for at least three glasses a day of fresh, cool water.

The question of drinking at meals should be decided by individuals or by the physician.

Fruit Beverages

These are excellent in warm weather and should be used freely. The standard lemonade is a good starting point, and one may vary combination of fruit juice, sugar and water, to give an almost endless variety of refreshing beverages.

Recipes

Lemonade

¼ cup lemon juice.
1 cup sugar.
1 pint water.

Boil sugar and water ten minutes. Add lemon juice; cool. Then add cold water to suit taste.

Orangeade

Make the same as lemonade.

Grape Juice

4 cups Concord grapes. $1\frac{1}{4}$ cup sugar. 1 pint water.

Wash grapes, remove stems, add water and cook one hour. Add sugar and cook thirty minutes longer. Strain, put into bottles and seal with sealing wax. When served, dilute with water, if desired.

Shrub

A pleasant summer drink is made by adding a few spoonfuls of fruit jelly to a glass of cool water. Stir until dissolved, and add sufficient quantity of jelly to suit taste. A good proportion is four tablespoonfuls jelly to each cup of water.

Hot Beverages

Simple heat has a slightly stimulating effect, and it is safer to depend on the simple hot drinks than upon alcoholic stimulants. The latter should never be given except in cases of shock or great exposure, nor should their use be continued even for a short time, except on advice of a physician.

The use of tea and coffee should never begin under twenty years of age, and even then a physician should decide as to whether they may be used safely.

Cocoa and chocolate are mildly stimulating, but the reaction is very slight.

Cereal Coffees

In preparing cereal coffees, it is quite safe to follow directions on package. Malt coffee should be ground before using.

Chocolate

1 ounce chocolate.
2 tablespoons sugar.
$\frac{1}{2}$ cup boiling water.
$1\frac{1}{2}$ cups hot milk and water.

Melt chocolate with sugar in double boiler, add boiling water, stirring constantly; cook directly over fire for five minutes, return to double boiler, cook twenty minutes and add hot milk and water.

Cocoa

2 level tablespoons cocoa.
1 of sugar.
Water to make thin paste.
1 cup boiling water.
1 cup hot milk, not boiling.

Stir cocoa and sugar to a paste with boiling water, add one cup of boiling water; cook directly over fire for five minutes, place in double boiler, cook twenty minutes, add hot milk and serve.

Cocoa Shells

½ cup shells.
3 cups cold water.

Let simmer for one hour, strain and serve.

Breakfast Coffee

5 level or 3 rounded tablespoons of coffee.
4 tablespoons cold water.
Shell of one egg or a little egg-white.
2½ cups water.
2 tablespoons cold water (for settling).

Stir to a paste the coffee, crushed eggshell or egg-white and the four tablespoons of cold water. Of the two and one-half cups of water, add one cup cold to coffee paste, bring to boiling, add remaining cup and one-half of water at boiling heat; let all boil three minutes and pour one tablespoon cold water down spout. Let stand to settle.

Tea

3 teaspoons tea.
2 cups boiling water.

Scald earthen or granite teapot, put in tea, add boiling water, remove to cool part of stove, steep three minutes only. Tea made with a tea ball at the table is particularly mild, and is the least harmful method of preparation.

After-Dinner Coffee

In black coffee use double the amount of coffee as that used for breakfast coffee.

Cereal Coffee

Malt coffee or any of the cereal coffees on the market make good tea and coffee substitutes for those to whom these are forbidden.

Directions: Follow all directions on package very carefully, although the strength may be varied to suit the taste.

Cocoa Shells and Coffee

For those who wish to decrease the strength of the coffee drunk, a very good combination is cocoa shells and coffee.

Directions: To each cup of coffee (p. 35) add one-half cup of cocoa shells (p. 35). This is good to break off the coffee habit gradually.

Cambric Tea for Children

1 cup milk.
1 cup hot water.
1 teaspoon sugar.
Speck of salt.

Heat milk, add hot water, salt and sugar. Serve very hot.

CHAPTER III

BREAD, BISCUITS, ROLLS, MUFFINS, ETC.

Bread Making

If the housekeeper is strong, she should make her own bread; and even if she has to consider her strength, it can be made easily with a bread-mixer.

Home-made bread is more nourishing than baker's bread.

General Remarks

Bread is raised either by yeast or baking powder. The actual process of leavening is somewhat complicated, and this chapter will discuss only the practical side.

The texture of the bread depends on the kneading. A fine-grained loaf is the result of thorough mixing.

Proportions

Liquid, 1 part.
Salt, ½ teaspoon to a loaf.
Sugar, ½ tablespoon to a loaf.
Flour, 3 to 4 parts.
Shortening, 1 tablespoon to a loaf.

Yeast

Set overnight, dough requires one-third cake to a pint of liquid.

Set in morning, dough will require one-half to one whole cake to each pint, according to time the bread is needed.

Mixing

The flour is beaten into the liquid, and the batter should be kept at an even consistency; when it becomes a dough, by the addition of more flour, it is turned out on a floured board and kneaded until firm and elastic. Only practice will give the "knack" of this.

Baking Powder Dough

The whole secret of baking powder biscuits is in very delicate handling. Toss with the finger tips only, and put out before cutting out biscuits.

Yeast Breads

White Bread

Rule—1 loaf:

- 1 cup lukewarm water.
- ½ teaspoon salt.
- ½ teaspoon sugar.
- ½ yeast cake.
- Flour to make soft dough.
- Part entire wheat if desired.

Dissolve yeast in a little lukewarm water; stir into one cup of water, also lukewarm, add salt and sugar, then gradually add flour, beating and then kneading to a soft dough. Let rise until it doubles in size, roll out air bubbles, shape into loaves, cover with melted fat, let rise one hour, then bake.

Bread Sticks

Form bread dough into finger rolls, let rise and bake. Good with soups.

Nut Bread

- 1 yeast cake.
- 1 cup scalded milk.
- 1 tablespoon sugar.
- ¾ cup chopped walnuts.
- 2 tablespoons lard.
- ⅓ cup sugar.
- White one egg.
- 3 cups flour.
- ⅓ teaspoon salt.

Dissolve yeast and sugar in milk, add one and a quarter cups flour, beat, cover. Let rise until light, add sugar and lard creamed, stiff white of egg, nuts, rest of flour and salt, knead, rise two hours or until light, mould, rise and bake forty-five minutes—one loaf.

Oatmeal Bread

2 cups boiling water.
2 cups rolled oats.
1 yeast cake.
¼ cup brown sugar.
4 cups flour.
1 teaspoon salt.

Pour two cups of boiling water over oatmeal, cover and let cool; add dissolved yeast and sugar; add one cup flour, beat, rise one hour; add flour for dough, then salt, let rise double, one and a half hours; mould, let rise an hour, bake forty-five minutes in hot oven.

Half cup chopped nuts and one tablespoon lard may be added.

Baking Powder Breads

Brown Bread

2 cups Graham flour.
1 cup white flour.
1 teaspoon soda.
1 teaspoon baking powder.
2 cups sour milk.
⅔ cup molasses.
1 teaspoon salt.

Mix and sift dry materials, add liquid materials and beat thoroughly. Bake in greased bread pan about one hour.

Baking Powder Biscuits

2 cups flour.
2 teaspoons baking powder.
½ teaspoon salt.
½ cup milk or water.
4 tablespoons lard.

Sift all dry materials together, chop in shortening, add liquid, pat out lightly and cut with floured glass. Bake in hot oven ten minutes.

Fruit Rolls

Spread out baking powder biscuit dough till one-fourth inch thick; sprinkle with sugar and cinnamon and currants; roll, cut into pieces about one and a half inches thick and bake in hot oven.

Graham Drop Cakes

Sift— { 1½ cups Graham flour.
½ teaspoon salt. }

½ teaspoon soda.
1 scant cup sour milk.
4 tablespoons sugar.

Mix into smooth batter. Drop by spoonfuls on buttered pan and bake fifteen minutes.

Fried Cakes

2 eggs.
1 cup sugar.
1 cup of milk.
Flour.

2 teaspoons baking powder rounded.
2 tablespoons lard.
Nutmeg.

Put one cup of flour in mixing bowl, add nutmeg and baking powder. Work in lard with finger tips; add sugar, eggs well beaten, milk and enough more flour to make a soft dough. Stir thoroughly and toss on a well-floured board. Knead slightly, using more flour if necessary. Pat and roll one to one-fourth inch thickness, shape and fry in deep fat according to directions for frying on page 74.

Short Cakes

Bake baking powder biscuit dough (p. 39) in thin sheets, put together with fillings of sweetened fruit, and a layer of fruit on top. For small cakes, use two cups flour.

Drop Biscuits

Follow the rule for baking powder biscuits on page 39, only add just enough liquid to make a dough that will drop from the spoon on hot muffin pans. Bake in moderate oven.

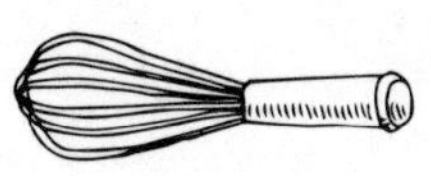

CHAPTER IV

BATTERS

Corn Meal Pan Cakes

4 tablespoons corn meal.
1 cup flour.
1½ teaspoons baking powder.
½ teaspoon salt.
¾ cup boiling water.
1 egg.
1 tablespoon sugar.
¾ cup milk.
1 tablespoon melted butterine.

Scald meal in boiling water, add milk and egg beaten together, then sifted dry materials, then butter, cook on greased griddle.

Plain Pan Cakes

1½ cup flour.
1½ teaspoon baking powder.
Small pinch salt.
1 tablespoon sugar.
1 cup milk.
1 egg.
1 tablespoon melted butterine.

Cook as other pan cakes.

Buckwheat Cakes

¼ yeast cake, dissolved in lukewarm water.
1 pint milk.

Buckwheat to make a pour batter (see p. 48).

Set overnight, then add two tablespoons molasses and one-quarter teaspoon soda. Beat together and cook on hot griddle.

Pop Overs

1 cup flour.
Small pinch salt.
1 cup half milk and half water.
1 egg.
3 tablespoons butterine.

Beat together and bake in greased muffin pans in moderate oven.

Plain Muffins

2 cups flour.
2 teaspoons baking powder.
Small pinch salt.
1 tablespoon butterine.
1 egg.
1 cup milk.

Sift all dry materials together, and beat into liquid. Bake in hot greased muffin pans.

Corn Pone

3 cups boiling water. 3 cups corn meal. Small pinch salt.

Stir together, spread evenly in a thin sheet on buttered pan and dot with bits of butterine and bake until brown.

Johnny Cake

½ cup milk.
1 cup corn meal.
1 cup flour.
2 tablespoons sugar.
3 teaspoons baking powder.
½ cup water.
Small pinch salt.
1 egg.
2 tablespoons melted dripping.

Beat together until smooth and bake in shallow pans.

Waffles

½ cup milk.
1 egg.
⅞ cup flour.
Small pinch salt.
½ tablespoon melted butterine.

Cook on hot, greased waffle iron.

Bread and Rice Pan Cakes

Either rice or soaked bread crumbs may be added to pancake batter, in the proportion of one cup of rice to seven-eighths cup of flour, with one cup of liquid, two eggs and a tablespoon of shortening—or one cup of crumbs to three-fourths cup of flour, one egg and one-half cup of liquid; the baking powder in either case being the usual rounded teaspoon to each cup.

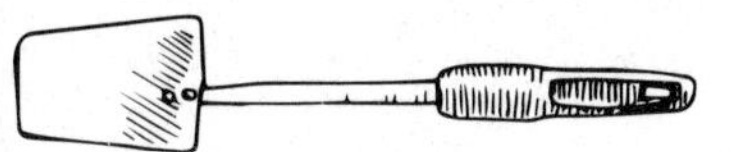  

CHAPTER V

CAKE

There are two general classes of cakes: sponge cakes and butter cakes. The former are made light by eggs and contain no shortening. The butter cakes vary in " richness " according to amount of shortening.

General Rules

In mixing butter cakes, cream butter very thoroughly.

Fold in whites of eggs last of all.

Do not " slam " oven door while cake is in oven.

Test cake by use of clean broom-straw. If straw comes out dry, if loaf shrinks from edge of pan, and if it " sings " with a slight hissing sound, the cake is done.

Turn from pan at once, and let cool without covering.

Dried fruit should be dredged with flour before adding to cake.

Baking Powder Sponge Cake

Beat { 2 eggs.
1 cup sugar.

Sift { 1 cup flour.
1½ teaspoon baking powder.
⅛ teaspoon suet.

Scant half cup hot water.

Beat sugar into yolks of eggs, add water and sifted dry materials. Fold in stiffly beaten whites and bake.

Black Chocolate Cake

½ cup butterine.
1½ cups sugar.
Yolk of 2 eggs.
2 cups flour.

1 teaspoon soda.
1 cup sweet milk.
¼ cake chocolate.
1 teaspoon vanilla.

Dissolve chocolate in milk, cool. Combine other materials as in one egg layer cake (page 45). This cake may be made either in loaf or layers.

Ginger Cookies

2 cups flour.	1 tablespoon ginger.
½ cup lard.	2 teaspoons soda.
1 cup molasses.	1 teaspoon salt.

Melt lard in hot molasses, stir in sifted dry material, roll out, cut out and bake—very little flour if necessary while shaping.

Harlequin Cake

½ cup butterine.	1 cup milk or water.
1½ cups sugar.	3 cups flour.
3 eggs.	3 teaspoons baking powder.

Combine materials as in rule for one egg layer cake (page 45). Divide mixture in three parts. To one add two squares of melted chocolate, to another a few drops of red vegetable coloring and the third leave plain. Bake in layers and put together with lemon dressing (page 47).

Hot Water Ginger Bread

1 cup of flour.	½ teaspoon ginger.
½ teaspoon soda.	½ cup of molasses.
¼ teaspoon salt.	¼ cup boiling water.
2 tablespoons melted drippings.	

Mix and sift dry materials, add molasses, water and drippings, beat, pour into a greased pan and bake twenty minutes in a moderate oven. This makes a small sheet of ginger bread.

Mechanics' Institute Cake

3 tablespoons butterine.	1½ teaspoons baking powder.
½ cup sugar.	5 tablespoons water.
1 egg-yolk.	1 egg-white.
1 cup flour.	½ teaspoon vanilla.

Cream butterine, add sugar gradually and egg-yolk beaten; sift flour and baking powder twice and add to mixture; add water, then egg-white beaten stiff and vanilla; bake half an hour in a moderate oven. This may be used for either loaf or layer cake (double rule) with any kind of frosting or filling. The above amount makes eight pieces when baked in a shallow tin. The addition of a sauce makes a good cottage pudding.

One Egg Layer Cake

1 tablespoon butter.
1 cup sugar.
1 egg.
1 teaspoon flavoring.
¾ cup milk or water.
1½ cup flour.
2 teaspoons baking powder.

Cream butter, add sugar gradually and egg slightly beaten; sift flour and baking powder together and add to mixture alternately with the milk. Vanilla, almond, lemon or other flavoring may be used. Bake in two layers in hot oven for about twenty minutes. (For frosting see page 47.)

Soft Molasses Cake

Put in a cup one tablespoon fat, three tablespoons hot water and fill the cup up with molasses. Use two cups of above, then add—

2 cups flour.
1 teaspoon soda.
1 teaspoon ginger.

Bake in moderate oven.

Sour Milk Ginger Bread

1 cup flour.
1 teaspoon soda.
¼ teaspoon salt.
2 tablespoons melted drippings.
1 teaspoon ginger.
½ cup molasses.
½ cup sour milk.

Mix and sift dry materials, add molasses, sour milk and drippings, beat mixture vigorously, pour into greased shallow pan and bake twenty minutes in a moderate oven.

Spice Cake without Eggs

1 cup sugar.
½ cup sour milk.
¾ cup flour.
½ cup shortening (butter, lard, dripping).
1 teaspoon soda.
2 teaspoons cinnamon.
1 teaspoon nutmeg.
Mix and sift together.

Cream shortening, add sugar gradually, then milk, flour and seasoning. Raisins or currants may be added, but it is not necessary. Bake in greased bread-pan in a moderate oven for about thirty minutes.

Sugar Cookies

For each cup of flour use one teaspoon baking powder, a few grains of salt, one-half cup sugar, two tablespoons shortening, one egg and one teaspoon vanilla, and two tablespoons milk. Cream sugar and butter, add egg, milk and flavoring. Then add sifted dry ingredients. Roll out, shape and bake.

White Cake

Put two egg-whites in a cup, fill cup until one-half full with melted butter, then put in enough milk to fill cup. Then add—

1 cup sugar.
1½ cups flour.
2 teaspoons baking powder.
1 teaspoon vanilla.

Beat mixture for five minutes. Bake in a loaf for thirty minutes in a moderate oven. The egg-yolks which are not called for in this cake may be used in making a custard or salad dressing.

Plain Boiled Frosting

1 egg-white.
½ teaspoonful vanilla.
¼ cup water.
½ cup sugar.

Boil sugar and water together until when dropped from spoon it forms a tiny thread. Beat egg-white until stiff and pour syrup on egg, slowly beating mixture with a fork or spoon until cool. Add flavoring. Cocoanut, chopped nuts or fruit may be added to the above for variety.

Chocolate Frosting

To plain boiled frosting add two squares of melted chocolate.

Chocolate Frosting, No. 2

¼ pound chocolate melted.
4 teaspoons butter.
⅓ cup hot water.
Powdered sugar—add enough to thicken.

Strawberry Frosting

½ cup sugar. 1 egg-white. 1 cup fresh strawberries.

Beat all together with whip.

Apple Frosting

1 egg-white. 1 apple (grate). 1 cup sugar.

Beat all till stiff.

Cream Caramel Frosting

6 tablespoons butter.
1½ cups sour cream or milk.
6 cups brown sugar.
1 teaspoon vanilla.

Cook to soft ball stage.

Lemon Dressing

3 tablespoons cornstarch.
4 tablespoons cold water.
½ teaspoon salt.
1 cup boiling water.
1 cup sugar.
2 tablespoons butter.
Juice of one lemon.
Grated rind of lemon.

Stir cornstarch and salt with cold water, pour on boiling water and cook on slow fire until mixture boils, stirring constantly. Add sugar, butter, lemon juice and rind.

Confectioners' Frosting

For an ordinary cake use two tablespoons boiling water; stir in enough confectioners' sugar to give a consistency that will spread. Flavor to suit taste.

MECHANICS' INSTITUTE TABLE

TABLE OF BATTERS AND DOUGHS

	Moisture to Flour 1 to 1			Moisture to Flour 1 to 2			
	Pour Batters.			Drop Batters—Muffins.			
	Popovers.	Griddle Cakes.	Waffles.	No Egg.	1 Egg.	Sour Milk.	Graham.
Milk, sweet	1 pt.	$^2/_3$ pt. (1 C.)	$^5/_8$ pt. (1 C.)	1 C.	1 C.		1 C.
Milk, sour						1 C.	
Melted Butter		1 tbsp. (¾ tbsp.)	1 tbsp. (2 tsp.)	3 tbsp.	3 tbsp.	2½ tbsp.	3 tbsp.
Pastry Flour	1 pt.	1 pt. (1½ c.)	1 pt. (1¾ c.)	2 c.	2 c.	2 c.	1 c.
Graham Flour							1 c.
Cornmeal							
Egg	3	2 small (1)	3 small (2)		1	1	1
Baking Powder		2 tsp. (1½ tsp.)	2 tsp. (1¾ tsp.)	4 tsp.	$3^1/_8$ tsp.	1½ tsp.	3½ tsp.
Soda						½ tsp.	
Salt	¼ tsp.	¼ tsp. ($^3/_{16}$ tsp.)	¼ tsp. ($^3/_{16}$ tsp.)	½ tsp.	½ tsp.	½ tsp.	½ tsp.
Sugar				2 tbsp.	½ tbsp.	½ tbsp.	
Molasses							2 tbsp.

MECHANICS' INSTITUTE TABLE

TABLE OF BATTERS AND DOUGHS

	Moisture to Flour 1 to 2				
	Muffins.	Corn Bread.		Fritters.	
	Cornmeal.	Johnny-cake.	Spider Custard.	Spoon.	
Milk, sweet	1 cup	1½ cups	1 cup		1 cup
Milk, sour			½ cup	1 cup	
Water				1½ cup	
Melted Butter	3 tbsp.	3 tbsp.	1½ tbsp.	2 tbsp.	
Pastry Flour	1⅓ cups	1 cup	¼ cup		2 cups
Cornmeal	⅔ cup	1 cup	¾ cup	1 cup	
Egg	1	1	1	1	1 large
Baking Powder	3½ tsp.	3 tsp.		¾ tsp.	3 tsp.
Soda			¼ tsp.	½ tsp.	
Salt	½ tsp.	½ tsp.	½ tsp.	½ tsp.	
Sugar	½ tbsp.	4 tbsp.	2 tbsp.		
Molasses				1 tbsp.	

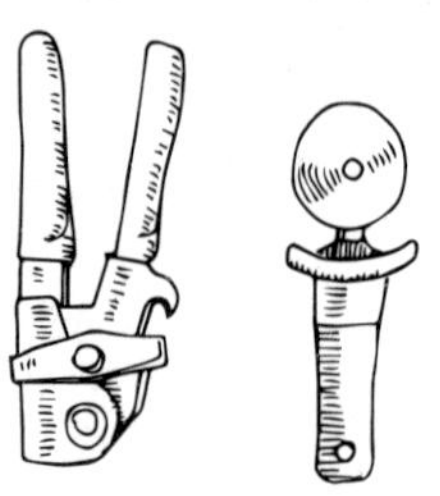

CHAPTER VI

CANNING AND PRESERVING

Canning is a method of keeping fruit by placing it in clean air-tight jars, and usually sugar is added. The amount of sugar used should be one-third the weight of the fruit and three cups of water to each pound of sugar.

Method

Make a thin syrup by boiling the sugar and water together for about ten minutes; then cook a small amount of fruit at a time in this syrup. Fill clean jars with fruit and add enough syrup to fill jars to overflowing. Place on rubber and screw on cover. Let stand until cool and tighten cover again.

To Clean Jars

1. Wash thoroughly and fill with cold water.
2. Place in large kettle filled with cold water.
3. Heat to boiling point, remove from fire and empty bottles.
4. Place covers in boiling water and let stand five minutes.
5. Dip rubbers in hot water.

Selection of Fruit for Canning

Fruit should be fresh, firm and not too ripe.

Canning of Vegetables

Prepare vegetables, place in jars and fill with cold water. Put on rubbers and cover, but not tightly. Place a towel in the bottom of a kettle and put jars on it. Fill kettle with cold water, bring to boiling point and boil one hour. Fill jars to overflowing with boiling water and fasten covers.

Jellies

The amount of sugar used in jelly-making is usually equal to the weight of fruit. Prepare fruit and place on fire; heat slowly to extract the juice. Spread sugar on a pan and heat in the oven. Add to fruit and boil about two minutes. Try a little on a cold saucer; as soon as it jellies it is cooked enough and is ready to pour into glasses. Let juice from juicy fruits cook about five minutes before adding sugar. Cover glasses with melted paraffin.

Preserving

When preserving fruit use from one-half to equal weight of sugar.

Orange Marmalade

4 large sour oranges.
3 lemons.
3½ pints cold water.
4 pounds granulated sugar.

Scrub fruit and cut in thin slices crosswise. Cover with cold water and let stand overnight. Simmer two hours, add sugar and cook one hour. Pour into glasses and cool. Seal.

Strawberry Preserve

Clean and hull berries and place in kettle, also an equal amount of sugar. Heat slowly and cook ten minutes. Remove skim. Place in clean jars and seal.

Suitable Fruits for Canning and Preserving

Cherries.
Peaches.
Plums.
Strawberries.
Blackberries.
Raspberries.
Pears.
Apricots.
Blueberries.
Rhubarb.
Pineapple.

The recipes in this chapter are given as illustrations.

CHAPTER VII

CASSEROLE COOKING

In the chapter on Fireless Cookers, it has been noted that very slow cooking will make tough meat tender and bring out the flavor of any food cooked in this way. The same principle is used in cooking in covered baking dishes. The casserole is the largest of these dishes, and beside this, we have ramequins or small covered dishes, egg shirrers and Dariole moulds or custard cups.

One advantage of this method is that food can be brought to the table in the same dishes as those used in cooking, and so it may be kept piping hot. The casserole may be placed in the outer plated cover before bringing it to the table.

Mixtures such as minced chicken and white sauce with beaten white of egg may be baked in small custard cups. These cups should be placed in a shallow pan of hot water (page 32).

Chicken En Casserole

Cut up a chicken as for fricassée, wipe each piece, sauté in butter until brown, place in casserole, cover with chicken stock or boiling water. Cover and bake one-half hour, then add a dozen slices of carrot and potato, five or six tiny onions browned in butter, seal dish with dough and bake half an hour longer, or until the vegetables are tender.

Braised beef (page 84) may be cooked deliciously in the casserole.

Lamb En Casserole

1 pound breast of lamb.	1 small onion.
½ cup tomatoes.	Water to half cover.

Cut meat in slices for serving, dredge with flour, add vegetables and water. Cover and cook two hours. Add one-quarter cup rice and, if necessary, more water; cover and cook another hour.

Vegetables En Casserole

Cut-up potatoes, celery, turnips or carrots may be browned in dripping, covered with brown gravy (page 82) and cooked in the casserole about three-quarters of an hour. Do not have too much of the gravy.

Shoulder Chops En Casserole

Prepare shoulder according to Lamb En Casserole and cook slowly in casserole for two hours.

Veal Chops

Cook the same as above.

Beef Heart En Casserole

Clean heart, plunge in boiling water, simmer for one hour, cut in slices, place in casserole, cover with strained and thickened tomato juice, cook two hours.

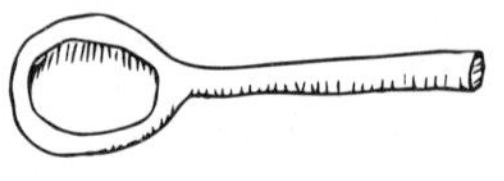

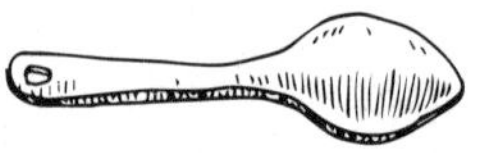

CHAPTER VIII

CEREALS

Points to Remember

1. Have water boiling.
2. Add salt.
3. Sift cereal in slowly.
4. Cook over fire until thickening begins.
5. Place kettle in large kettle containing boiling water and cook several hours, according to the kind. It may be cooked overnight or in fireless cooker (p. 25).
6. Different kinds of cereals need different amounts of water. A general rule is two and a half times as much water as grain, and a teaspoon of salt for every quart of water.

Chopped dates, figs or raisins may be added to cooked mush. This makes a good dessert.

Table for Cereals

	Grain	Water	
1 cup	Rolled oats	2 cups.	Time for cooking at least one hour, the longer the better, except in the case of rice which should boil rapidly for twenty minutes.
	Cornmeal	6 cups.	
	Hominy	4 cups.	
	Farina	2 cups.	
	Cream of wheat	2 cups.	
	Pettijohn's	2 cups.	
	Rice	6 cups.	

Cereal Moulded with Fruit

Any cereal may be made more appetizing and attractive by the addition of various fruits, raw or stewed. When the cereal has been cooked, it may be put in a cup and allowed to cool. Then turn it out on to a cereal dish and surround with stewed prunes, apricots or apple sauce, sliced bananas or fresh fruit in season.

Fried Mush

Cold cornmeal or any other mush may be sliced, dipped in flour and browned in frying pan with dripping. This is excellent with molasses, syrup or butter.

Cereal with Dates

2 cups cooked mush. ½ cup chopped dates.

Cook together until dates are thoroughly soft.

Cereal with Raisins

Cook as above, only in place of dates add one-half cup chopped raisins.

Cereal Puddings

Cold cereal may be reheated, sweetened to taste, chopped fruit added, with a beaten egg with milk to give lightness. The whole is then dotted with butterine and baked.

Cereal Gems

Use cold cooked mush, stir in a very little sugar and enough beaten egg and milk to make a soft mixture. Bake in hot muffin pans. If light gems are desired, use a teaspoon of baking powder sifted with half cup of flour for each cup of mush.

CHAPTER IX

CHAFING DISH COOKERY

Anything that can properly be cooked in a double boiler can be prepared in a chafing dish. To use this successfully, it is necessary to understand the cooking of food over hot water (see page 32).

The greatest care must be taken in the use of a chafing dish, to prevent accidents—in filling and handling. The chafing dish should rest on a metal tray.

Rules

Creamed Dishes

Make a thin white sauce (page 32) and serve with flaked cold fish, oysters, peas, lobster, chicken or anything desired.

Egg Dishes

Eggs may be hard boiled, cut up and creamed, or scrambled and served with grated cheese, or with tomato sauce.

Warmed Over Dishes

Corned Beef Hash

Equal parts of chopped cold corned beef and potato. Place in blazer over the hot water pan, moisten with milk and brown with a little butter.

Minced Meat on Toast

Use cold steak or roast beef, put through meat chopper, season nicely, add a little chopped onion, or shredded peppers, tomato or anything fancied. Place in blazer, cover with brown gravy (see page 86) and heat thoroughly. Serve on toast.

Young housekeepers are advised, if they use a chafing dish, to stick to plain creamed dishes and warmed over dishes, like those outlined above, rather than to attempt elaborate combinations that require much butter and other expensive additions.

The remarks on seasoning (page 29) apply equally here, for everyone has a chance to give real character to a dish by a little care.

Dried Beef

Pick up one cup dried beef, cover with tomato sauce, add one tablespoon butter, heat and stir in three beaten eggs. Cook until eggs are creamy.

Omelet with Cheese

For a medium size omelet use two eggs, season with salt and pepper, add three teaspoons melted butter and two teaspoons grated cheese. Cook until firm. Sprinkle with grated cheese.

Chafing Dish Rarebit

For each cup of hot milk use a scant cup of crumbs. Soak these in the milk, then add two teaspoons melted butterine, one-half cup of cheese chopped fine; then stir in an egg, after white and yolk have been beaten separately. Add yolk before taking from stove, and white after removing.

French Toast

4 slices stale bread.
2 eggs.
1 tablespoon sugar.
¾ cup milk.
⅛ teaspoon salt.

Beat eggs, milk, sugar and salt together. Dip slices of bread in this and brown on greased pan.

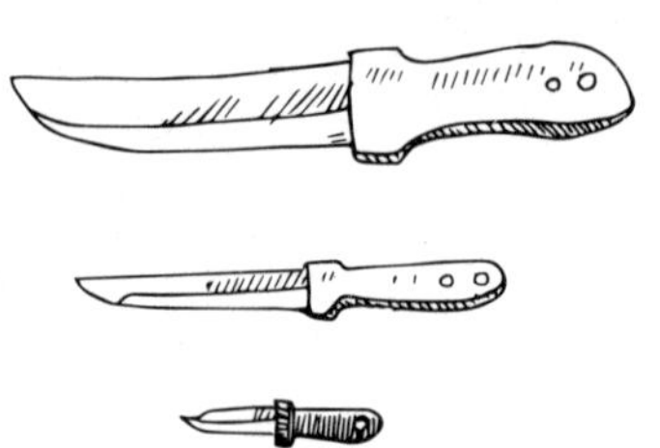

CHAPTER X

CHEESE

A SMALL piece of cheese contains a large amount of nourishment, and if cheese is used wisely it is a valuable food. The mistake made by many is that of eating cheese in large quantities, at the same meal with other "hearty" food.

This is especially true if cheese is eaten raw, for it is then masticated more or less imperfectly and the stomach has too much work to do.

How to Use Cheese

If eaten in any quantity, cheese should form the chief dish of a meal at luncheon or supper; it may be eaten uncooked in sandwiches, or it may be grated or chopped very fine and stirred very slowly into hot cereals or used on toast, etc.

Cereal and Cheese

2 cups boiling water.
½ teaspoon salt.
¼ pound grated cheese.
⅓ cup fine grained cereal.
(Cornmeal, hominy, cream of wheat, etc.)

Stir chopped or grated cheese slowly into hot cereal.

Cheese Fondu

1 cup milk.
1 cup bread crumbs.
¾ cup grated cheese.
1 egg.
Salt, pepper and mustard.

Soak bread crumbs in milk, heat, add cheese, season, and when cheese is melted and stirred through the crumbs, add beaten egg and remove from fire. Spread on crackers or toast. This is the most wholesome form of rarebit.

Cheese Pudding

Fill a small pudding dish as follows:

Dip slices of bread in milk and egg beaten together, place a layer of this soaked bread in the pan, sprinkle with a thick layer of grated cheese; add another layer of soaked bread, and so on until the dish is filled. Bake in slow oven until firm.

Cheese Toast

4 slices of toast.
¼ pound grated cheese.

Sprinkle cheese on toast, place slices on tin plate and leave in oven until cheese is melted. Serve very hot.

Creamed Macaroni

½ pound boiled macaroni.
3 cups white sauce.
2 tablespoons flour.
¼ pound cheese.

Thicken milk with flour, rubbed to a paste in a little cold water. Chop cheese very fine and stir slowly through the hot sauce.

Hominy Baked with Cheese

Prepare boiled hominy in the ordinary way, stir grated cheese (one-quarter pound to two cups of cooked mush) through while hot, make into mound, dot with butter, and brown in oven.

Rarebit

½ pound cheese.
½ cup milk.
½ teaspoon cornstarch.
1 tablespoon butter.
Salt, pepper and mustard to taste.

Blend butter and cornstarch, add milk, then cheese and seasonings. Stir until cheese is smooth. Serve on crackers.

Rice and Cheese with Brown Gravy

½ cup rice.
¼ pound grated cheese.
2 cups brown gravy. (See page 86.)

Boil rice rapidly in three cups of water, stir cheese through slowly, so that heat of rice will melt it, pour on brown gravy and serve very hot. This is a nourishing substitute for meat.

Cheese Crackers

6 crackers.
10 tablespoons grated cheese.

Place crackers in shallow pan, sprinkle cheese on top and bake until cheese melts.

Cheese Porridge

Stir grated cheese through any hot cooked mush. A good way to use up dry bits of cheese, as even a little increases food value of the mush.

Cheese Custard

Prepare baked custard mixture (p. 95) and sprinkle top with grated cheese before baking.

Grated Cheese

Grate Roman cheese and pass with plain rice or macaroni.

Cheese Balls

Make tiny balls of soft cheese and serve with salad.

CHAPTER XI

CONFECTIONS

PURE candy is wholesome if not eaten in excess. With fondant as a foundation great variety of cream candy can be made, by using different flavors, adding nuts, etc.

Chocolate Caramels

2 cups sugar.
4 cups molasses.
1 cup milk.
6 ounces chocolate.
2 teaspoons vanilla.
4 tablespoons butterine.

Melt butter, add molasses, sugar and milk; when it boils add chocolate, and stir until melted; boil until a soft ball can be formed. Add vanilla, remove from fire, pour into buttered pan, cool and mark in squares.

Fondant

2 cups granulated sugar.
1 cup hot water.
⅓ teaspoon cream of tartar.

Set kettle on cool part of stove and stir only until sugar is dissolved. Boil rapidly until a little dropped into cold water will form a soft ball. Remove from fire and cool in kettle in which it has been cooked. When cool, stir until creamy, then knead with the hands, cover with a damp cloth and let stand until ready for use. It will be better after standing two or three days.

Fudge

1 cup white sugar.
1 cup brown sugar.
1 cup milk.
4 squares chocolate.
2 tablespoons butter.
Vanilla, raisins or nut meats if desired.

Boil all together until a soft ball will form in cold water;

then beat until creamy, pour on buttered platter, cool and mark in squares.

Maple Sugar Candy

½ pound maple sugar.
6 tablespoons thin cream.
2 tablespoons boiling water.
½ cup nut meats cut in pieces.

Put sugar, cream and water into a saucepan and boil until when tested in cold water a soft ball is formed. Remove from fire, beat until creamy, add nuts. Pour into a buttered pan. Cool and mark in squares.

Peanut Taffy

1 quart peanuts.
2 cups sugar.

Melt sugar, and stir in chopped nuts which have been salted. Pour on buttered plate.

Taffy

1 cup sugar.
4 tablespoons vinegar.
1 tablespoon butter.

Melt butter, add sugar and vinegar and stir until sugar is dissolved. Boil until when tried in cold water mixture will be brittle. Turn out on a buttered plate to cool. Pull and cut in pieces.

Caramel for Flavoring

Equal parts of sugar and boiling water.

Melt sugar in smooth omelet pan, stirring until it is brown, add water and cook slowly for twelve minutes.

Old Time Molasses Candy

1 pint dark molasses.
3 tablespoons butterine.
⅔ cup sugar.
2 teaspoons vinegar.

Boil until a bit dropped in cold water will snap. When nearly done add vinegar and stir constantly. Pour on buttered plate, cool and pull.

CHAPTER XII

DECORATIONS

The setting of an attractive table has already been spoken of, but the tasteful garnishing of the food itself is equally important.

When one can spend only a limited amount of money, it may not seem worth while to attempt the graceful touches that add so much to the pleasure of a meal, but this is a wrong idea. With scrupulous cleanliness as a foundation, one may take the next step, that is, an attempt to provide real charm, and this beauty touch has a decided effect on digestion, and consequently on health.

A Few Simple Hints

For two cents one can buy enough parsley to make the cheapest of shoulder chops look as dainty as those from the loin, to give flavor and character to the potato and other cream soup, to " dress up " a plain potato salad, to beautify the white sauce of left over fish, or for any of the other numberless uses to which a bit of green may be put.

A plain cornstarch pudding may be moulded and served with a candied cherry on top of each mould.

A salmon loaf is quite beautiful if served with a border of ordinary canned peas.

Prosaic stews look attractive if the accompanying or boiled rice is carefully arranged in a border around the meat, instead of being served in a separate dish. Numerous modifications of the border idea are possible—combining diced carrots and peas for a meat loaf, etc.

Everyone remembers his childish enjoyment of colored sugar on small cakes, or anything that gave a spice of novelty. The housekeeper should remember that no one ever outgrows entirely this pleasure in the novel or unexpected, so that when she bakes she may produce all manner of pretty effects with white and chocolate frosting, strawberry and lemon ice, etc.

The more delicate flowers can always be used to advantage in decoration and a plain cake fairly bloom out from a wealth of green leaves.

So simple a matter as the placing of wafers or small cakes on the plate gives an opportunity to produce a good effect. Instead of a jumbled heap, long, narrow wafers may be placed to resemble the radiating spokes of a wheel, with a tiny round cake at the center.

These few hints are given merely to show the housekeeper that it is worth while to put a little effort into the simplest of everyday matters, and to remind her that she will have her reward in the increased contentment and health of her family.

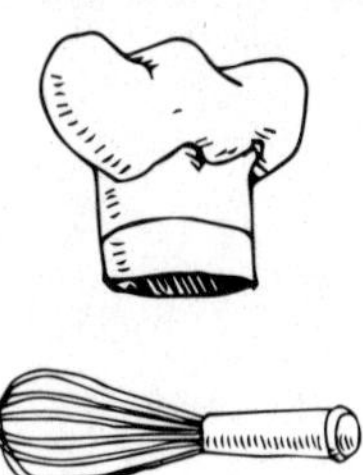

CHAPTER XIII

EGGS

Boiled Eggs

The proper term is "cooked eggs," as it is important that eggs should not be boiled, but merely cooked in the steam of water that is at boiling point. In this way the white will be tender and jelly-like; the firmness may be regulated by length of time the egg remains in the water.

Rule.—Wash eggs and place in saucepan of boiling water, cover, and move to cool part of stove where the water will not boil.

Time in Water

Soft egg	5 minutes.	Hard egg	30 minutes.
Medium egg	7 "		

Creamy or Coddled Egg

For each beaten egg used, one-third cup of milk; season with salt and pepper; cook in double boiler until thick and creamy. Serve on toast.

Use great care to see that the water in under part of boiler does not boil rapidly, as this would cause the white to harden, just as in the case of "boiled eggs."

Fried Eggs

Break eggs, one at a time, in a saucer, have bacon fat melted in hot omelet pan, slip eggs in carefully, and dip hot fat over them, as water is used in poaching eggs.

Scrambled Eggs

This rule follows naturally the rule for creamy egg, as the consistency in each case is about the same, although the method is different.

Rule.—For each egg use a tablespoon of milk; separate white and yolk, beat yolks lightly, add milk, salt and pepper, beat whites until firm and fold into mixture.

Have omelet pan hot with two tablespoons of melted butter (for four eggs), pour in mixture, place on stove and stir with fork as it thickens, and continue until soft and creamy. Lift pan from fire occasionally if heat is too great.

Omelet Plain

3 eggs.
3 tablespoons milk.
Salt and pepper.

Beat all together, pour into buttered omelet pan, brown on under side, fold and turn out on smoking hot platter.

Suggestions to Vary Omelets

Sprinkle in grated cheese before folding.

Sprinkle in grated ham.

Sprinkle in mixture of cooked vegetables.

Spread with jelly.

Sprinkle with minced parsley.

Add chopped raw peppers which have been cooked in butter until soft.

Poached Egg

Break egg in a saucer, slip carefully into pan containing simmering water. Dip water over egg occasionally, cook until white is firm, and remove to slices of toast.

General Remarks

Eggs may be cooked hard and served in white sauce (page 32).

They may be cut up and used cold in salads.

They may be served with tomato sauce, and in short they may be used in almost endless variety, to suit individual taste.

Stuffed Eggs

3 hard-cooked eggs.
1 cup white sauce.
Seasoning to taste.

Cut eggs in halves lengthwise, take out yolks and mix smooth with milk and seasoning and chopped parsley, return to whites and serve with white sauce.

Baked Eggs

Prepare above and place in small pudding dish, cover with crumbs and brown in oven.

Egg Timbales

Prepare a firm, baked custard (p. 95) and cook in small cups set in pan of water.

CHAPTER XIV

FISH

The old-fashioned idea, that of fish being a "brain food" no longer prevails, but it is known that because fish is more quickly digested than some forms of meat, it furnishes acceptable variety to diet, especially the diet of sedentary persons. The flesh of some fish, the so-called "white fishes," is less fat throughout than that of the oily fishes.

Below is a list of common fish used for food:

Bass.
Cod.
Crawfish.
Bluefish.
Flounder.
Finnan Haddie (dried).
Haddock.
Herring (smoked).
Porgies.
Salmon.
Shad.
Smelts.
Trout (fresh water).
Mackerel.
White fish.

To Select Fish

See that flesh is firm and that the eyes and gills are bright.

Shell Fish

Clams.
Oysters.
Scallops.
Crabs.
Shrimps.
Lobsters.

Preparation of Fish for Cooking

Remove scales by scraping toward head.

Clean inside.

Cut skin near on the back, remove skin on each side, pulling toward tail.

To bone—After skinning, take flesh from backbone from one side, then from the other.

Baked Canned Salmon

Pick up fish, remove all hard bits, add equal parts of bread crumbs, moisten with an egg beaten in a little milk, having mass of the right consistency to form a smooth loaf in pudding pan, season, add chopped parsley, make into mound in baking pan, brown in oven. Crumbs dotted with bits of butter may be spread on top before browning.

Baked Fish

Spread some butter over an agate dripping-pan or cover with thin slices of fat salt pork. Sprinkle over it one onion minced fine. Lay on this a thin slice of halibut or any small, whole fish split down the middle. Add one tablespoon vinegar, and spread thickly with butter and flour rubbed together. Bake until done, the time depending upon the thickness of the fish. When the pan is buttered or pork laid under the fish, it may be easily removed with a flexible knife. Or a strip of cheesecloth or tough greased paper may be put underneath and be drawn out with the fish.

Boiled Fish

Fish for boiling should either be wrapped in cheesecloth or cut in slices and placed very carefully in the water to keep it from falling to pieces. Care should be taken not to cook fish too long or it will become tough. Boiled fish needs highly flavored sauces in order to make it palatable. The best kinds of fish for boiling are the so-called white varieties. Several authorities call attention to the fact that this is an extravagant way of cooking fish, unless the liquor is used, as in a fish stock.

Broiled Fish

Remove head, tail and fins and split. Remove backbone from cod or haddock; cut large fish into inch slices. Brush fish and broiler with melted fat. Broil the flesh side until brown, then turn the skin toward the coal; or, with a gas stove, put broiler in pan in the upper oven for the last five minutes. Cook from ten to twenty minutes, according to thickness.

Steamed Clams

Wash shells well, scrubbing and changing water until it is absolutely clean. Place in kettle with one cup of hot water for half a peck, cover and steam until shells open slightly, remove from shells, pour liquor very carefully into a bowl or saucepan, strain, serve hot with butter. Serve this hot broth with the clams.

Fried Clams

Use steamed clams, remove from shell, rinse, dip in batter and fry. (See page 31.)

Codfish Hash

1 cup salt fish, shredded.
2 cups diced boiled potatoes.
½ teaspoon pepper.
½ tablespoon melted dripping.

Mash potatoes, stir into fish, place in pan with enough melted fat to moisten mixture, heat thoroughly, brown on both sides and serve. Codfish should always be freshened by pouring on boiling water until salt is washed out. Do not soak nor boil.

Creamed Codfish

1 pound salt cod.

Pick up codfish, freshen by pouring on boiling water; do not soak. When fish is freshened to suit taste, place it in pan, sprinkle with flour, cover with cold milk, cook, stirring constantly until soft and thick; season.

Crabs

Hard-Shelled Crabs.—The meat may be seasoned, chopped and made into a variety of dishes—creamed, patties, etc.

Soft-Shelled Crabs.—Never use unless alive. Remove spongy part and pouch, rinse and use like lobster, oysters and clams.

Shrimps

Use like lobster in a sauce or made into salad.

Creamed Fish

For each cup of white sauce (page 32) use one and three-quarters cups of cold, flaked fish. Season with salt and pepper, minced onion if liked, and chopped parsley.

This may be made into scalloped fish by placing in an oiled baking dish, and covering with buttered crumbs. Place the pan in the oven until the crumbs are brown.

Fish-balls

Freshen salt codfish by placing the shredded fish in a colander and pouring boiling water through it until the salt is sufficiently washed away. For every cup of salt codfish allow two cups of mashed potato, half-tablespoon of melted dripping, one beaten egg, and pepper to taste. This may be made into fish-balls and browned in a frying-pan, or made into a large cake, the size of the pan, and browned first on one side and then on the other—this saves time and fat.

Fried Oysters and Clams

Dip in batter (page 74) and fry in deep fat.

Broiled Oysters

Dip large oysters in melted butter; season with salt and pepper and then in fine cracker crumbs. Put on buttered broiler and cook five minutes or more until the juice begins to run.

Lobster

Lobster may be served plain or made into fancy dishes, such as croquettes. It should be cooked just long enough to heat, or it will be tough.

Creamed Lobster

½ cup minced lobster.
White of egg.
½ tablespoon flour.
½ tablespoon butterine.
Salt and pepper.
⅓ cup milk.
Yolk of one egg.

Cook lobster with butter five minutes, add flour, seasoning, yolk of egg, then stiffly beaten white of egg. Bake in custard cups in pan of hot water. (See page 32.)

Kippered Herring

Remove fish from can and arrange on plate that may be put in the oven; sprinkle with pepper, brush over with lemon juice and a very little melted butter. Pour over the liquor left in the can. Heat thoroughly and garnish with parsley and slices of lemon.

Scallops

These may be creamed, fried or made into soup.

To Prepare

Rinse scallops, parboil in their own juice and drain.

Sauce

Thicken the liquor with butter and flour cooked together. Season, pour over scallops in a baking dish, cover with crumbs and bake until brown.

Scalloped Oysters

1 pint oysters.
4 tablespoons oyster liquor.
2 tablespoons milk.
½ cup stale bread crumbs.
1 cup cracker crumbs, buttered.
Salt and pepper to taste.

Mix bread and cracker crumbs. Put a thin layer in the bottom of a shallow baking dish, then add a layer of oysters. Season with salt and pepper. Moisten with part of the liquor and milk, add another layer of crumbs, alternating with oysters, and bake about half an hour with a layer of crumbs on top.

Creamed Oysters

For each pint of oysters use a cup and a half of white sauce (page 32) and an eighth of a teaspoon of celery salt.

Pigs in Blankets

Select large oysters, clean, wrap a thin slice of bacon around each oyster, fasten with a wooden toothpick and bake in pan.

Planked Fish

Use a smooth plank about 2 inches thick. Split fish, place on plank with skin side down. Butter lightly and season with salt and pepper. Bake about half an hour. Serve from plank.

Finnan Haddie

Parboil five minutes; and serve with a thin, white sauce, or broil as if fresh.

Sauce for Baked Fish

1 teaspoon butterine.
1 egg yolk.
1 teaspoon vinegar.
Salt.
Pepper.
Lemon juice.
2 tablespoons boiling water.

Melt butterine, beat in egg yolk, seasoning, boiling water and vinegar. Cook over hot water until thick, then add lemon juice, three or four drops.

CHAPTER XV

FRYING

Use Tests for Fat (page 31)

Food must be dipped in rolled crumbs, then beaten egg (diluted with one tablespoon water), then in crumbs again.

Fritters

Slice any desired fruit, dip in batter and fry in deep fat.

Batter

1 cup flour.
1 egg.
1 teaspoon baking powder.
½ cup milk.
⅛ teaspoon salt.

Mashed Potato Cakes

Mashed potato moistened with white sauce, and made into flat cakes may be sautéd, or it may be dipped in egg and crumbs and fried.

Meat Croquettes

One and three-quarter cups cold fowl or lamb or roast beef, cut in food chopper, season with one-half teaspoon salt, one-quarter teaspoon celery salt, one teaspoon chopped parsley, few drops onion juice. Add one cup thick white sauce (page 32), shape, crumb and fry. Serve with tomato sauce (page 119) or brown sauce (page 86).

Vegetable Croquettes

Any mashed vegetable may be made into croquettes—potato, parsnips, etc.

Rice Croquettes

½ cup milk.
¼ cup rice (cooked).
½ teaspoon salt.
1 egg-yolk.
½ tablespoon butterine.

Cook rice, then add milk and other ingredients, shape, crumb and fry. Serve with jelly.

To Shape Croquettes

Have ready some beaten egg on a plate, and on another some finely rolled cracker dust. After croquette mixture is well blended, flour hands very lightly, take up a good tablespoonful, roll it on board with palm of hand until it resembles a small sausage; with tips of fingers flatten both ends, then dip croquette in egg, then crumbs, then egg, and fry in deep fat.

CHAPTER XVI

FRUITS

Fruits are one of the most important articles of food, and if rightly used add much to the healthfulness of the diet. The common idea that they are indigestible, comes from the habit of eating them at the end of a hearty meal when the stomach is already overtaxed.

The best time to eat fruit is in the morning or at luncheon. However, if the evening meal is a light supper, stewed fruit is an excellent addition.

Serving of Fruits

Apples are very wholesome eaten raw. The skins should be washed, then removed, and the apple thoroughly masticated.

Apple Compote

Pare apples, cut in quarters, stew in a syrup made of equal parts of sugar and water; cook until quite tender, but see that each piece keeps its shape. Remove carefully to a pretty dish, then boil down syrup until thick and pour over apples.

Apple Sauce

Pare apples, stew until tender with sugar according to variety of apple, and a very little water. Mash and strain through a colander.

Baked Apples

Wash and core apples, fill cavities with sugar and cinnamon mixed, stick blanched almonds in top of apples, place in shallow pan and bake until soft.

Bananas

These are a cheap and valuable food if they are well selected, and properly prepared for the table. Bananas are **not** ripe until the skin is decidedly dark.

To prepare, remove skin, scrape banana lightly to remove the irritating stringy part next the skin, then cut up and serve with milk and sugar or with lemon juice and sugar.

Baked Bananas

Place in shallow pan, cover pan and bake until skins are very dark. Remove skins and sprinkle with powdered sugar.

Sautéd Bananas

Remove skins, cut in halves, dip in flour and cook in butter in a frying pan. Serve hot, sprinkled with sugar.

Berries

Clean thoroughly and serve with powdered sugar.

Dates

Dates are nourishing and may be chopped and added to cereals, or stewed in double boiler, or made into sandwiches between sweet crackers.

Quinces

Quinces and pears may be served baked.

Quinces may be used for jelly and marmalade.

Dried Fruit

This may be used for puddings or pies.

Raisins make a good sauce if stewed until soft.

Fruit Toast

Stewed berries poured hot over slices of toast make a delicious breakfast or supper dish.

Grapefruit

Wipe fruit and cut in halves crosswise. Use a sharp knife and separate each section of pulp from the tough white skin. Let stand for ten minutes, sprinkled with powdered sugar.

Oranges

To serve, wipe fruit and cut in halves, crosswise—place on plate with spoon.

If served cut up, remove all white skin before cutting.

Stewed Prunes

Wash thoroughly. Cook in cold water two or three hours; cook until very tender. Add a little sugar and a few teaspoons of lemon juice.

Stewed Rhubarb

Peel and cut rhubarb into inch bits, sprinkle with sugar, add just enough water to prevent burning and cook until soft.

Fruit Dessert

2 bananas.
1 orange.
Sugar.
Whipped cream.

Cut orange and bananas, add sugar and cream. Serve in sherbet cups.

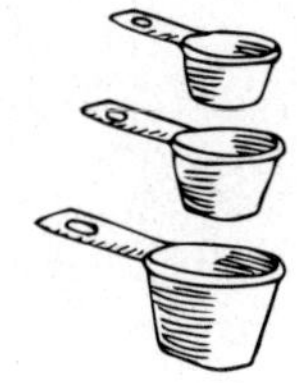

CHAPTER XVII

FROZEN DESSERTS

Use rock salt, and in packing freezer use one part crushed ice to three of salt.

Chocolate Ice Cream

Two squares of chocolate, one cup of sugar and one teaspoon vanilla to each quart of cream.

Chocolate Sauce for Ice Cream

To each square of chocolate use one-half cup water, two teaspoons butter and a few drops of vanilla. Blend all smoothly and cook in double boilers.

Fruit Cream

Use any crushed fruit and stir into plain ice cream.

Philadelphia Ice Cream

This is the simplest ice cream, being simply thin cream, sweetened, flavored and frozen.

Water Ices

Sweeten and add fruit juice to water, allowing two cups of sugar for each quart of water. Proportions: three-fourths cup lemon juice or two cups berry juice to one quart water.

To Freeze Any Mixture Without a Freezer

Place mixture in a small granite pail, place pail in larger pail, with layer of chopped ice under inside pail, then pack space between pails with coarse salt and chopped ice, three cups of ice for each cup of salt. Turn inner pail constantly until mixture begins to freeze, then scrape from sides of pail, continue freezing, scrape again, and so on until thick.

Ice Cream with Gelatine

2 cups thin cream.
1 cup milk.
1 cup sugar.
1 tablespoon gelatine.

Dissolve gelatine in boiling water, combine all ingredients, flavor with fruit juice. Freeze.

Banana Ice Cream

Stir mashed bananas through a plain ice cream mixture until it is of consistency of thick cream. Freeze. Proportions: Four bananas to each quart of cream.

Frozen Custard

4 eggs.
1 quart milk.
1 cup sugar.
Flavoring to suit taste.

Make a boiled custard (page 97). Mould and chill.

Caramel Ice Cream

3 cups milk and cream.
1 egg.
½ cup sugar.
2 teaspoons vanilla.
1 tablespoon flour.

Caramel (page 62)

½ cup sugar.
Brown in smooth pan.

Scald milk, thicken with flour, add sugar and beaten egg. Cook half an hour, add caramel, cool and freeze.

CHAPTER XVIII

MACARONI AND OTHER ITALIAN PASTES

MACARONI, spaghetti and the other Italian pastes are valuable food, if properly used. The imported macaroni and some of that made in this country is made of flour that contains a large amount of nourishment, but some of the American macaroni is made of flour from soft wheat, and is mostly starch.

Cooking of Italian Pastes

All the pastes, whether it be the tiny noodles used in soup or the coarser forms of spaghetti and macaroni, should be put into actively boiling water. Otherwise they will be pasty and sticky. The fine forms are used chiefly in soups, while many appetizing dishes can be made from spaghetti and macaroni.

Baked Macaroni with Cheese

½ cup macaroni.
2 tablespoons butterine.
¼ cup grated cheese.
Salt and pepper.
Milk to cover.

Butter a pudding pan, put in a layer of cooked macaroni, sprinkle with grated cheese, add another layer of macaroni, and so on until pan is nearly full. On top dot with bits of butter. Over all pour milk to nearly cover. Bake until cheese is melted.

Macaroni may also be baked with alternate layers of chopped hard boiled eggs. Pour over white sauce to cover and leave in oven just long enough to heat thoroughly.

Creamed Macaroni and Cheese

Macaroni and tomato prepare the same as above, using strained, hot stewed tomato in place of milk in the sauce (see page 32).

Macaroni with Oysters

2 cups macaroni.
1 cup white sauce.
1 cup oysters.

Mix all together, cover with bread crumbs and bake until brown.

Macaroni—Creole Style

1 cup macaroni.
4 tablespoons grated cheese.
3 tomatoes.
½ pound chopped meat.
Salt and pepper.
Small slice onion.

Boil macaroni with cut-up tomato and onion, brown meat in a little suet, add this and the cheese to macaroni and cook until cheese melts. In browning the meat add boiling water enough to make a brown sauce to serve with this dish.

Scalloped Macaroni

Place a layer of cooked macaroni in a small pudding dish. Pour over strained tomato juice, sprinkle with finely grated cheese, add another layer of macaroni and so on until the dish is nearly full, and for the top layer sprinkle stale bread crumbs dotted with tiny bits of butter. See that the dish has enough of the tomato juice poured through it and around it to thoroughly moisten all layers. Place in oven and brown crumbs.

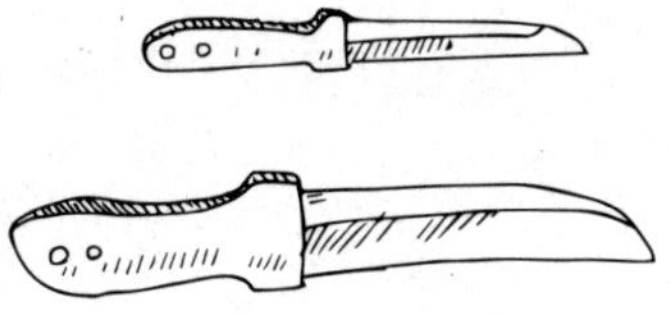

CHAPTER XIX

MEAT—GAME—POULTRY

How to Cook Meat

THE object of cooking meat is to make it tender and to keep in the juice and preserve the flavor. To keep in the juice and preserve the flavor, sear the meat on both sides; that is, press it down quickly on a hot pan, and then turn and sear the other side. When the meat turns a whitey brown color, a coating has been formed which will keep in the juice. After searing the meat cook it slowly unless it is broiled. This will make it tender. Beef and mutton are the meats that are best for all persons.

To make soup one must draw out the juice. To do this, place the meat in cold water, bring to boiling point and cook gently until tender.

Wipe meat with wet cloth; do not wash in cold water, as this will draw out and waste the juice.

Do not add salt to raw meat as it draws out the juice. Add it while cooking.

For stew plunge meat in cold water, bring quickly to boiling point and let simmer, *not boil*, until tender.

For pot roast, put meat into boiling water, then let simmer.

To Broil Chops or Steak

Wipe meat with a cloth wrung out of cold water, place on greased broiler and sear on one side, then turn and sear on the other. This is done by holding very near the fire, and when the red color disappears, it is a sign that the juices are sealed up. The meat can then be browned on each side, sprinkled with salt, spread with a small bit of butter and removed to a very hot platter. Do not add salt until the meat has been seared, as this will draw out the juice.

If one has not a wire broiler, the meat can be pan-broiled on a sizzling hot, oiled frying pan. Enough fat will cook out of ordinary meat to finish the cooking without the addition of more fat.

Beef Cutlets Braised

(Miss Barrows.)

Cut any inexpensive meat in pieces for serving, cover with brown gravy, bake in covered dish until meat is tender. Flank or chuck will do for this.

Beef's Liver

Cut in one-half inch slices, place in boiling water for ten minutes, drain, remove skin, dip in melted pork or bacon fat, and broil or fry.

Beef Loaf

Chopped meat (one-half pound) and equal parts of moistened bread crumbs, one small onion, salt and pepper. Mix all together and place in hot greased baking pan and bake about one hour or until well browned. Serve with brown gravy or tomato sauce.

Boiled Ham

Ham should be soaked overnight in cold water to cure. Drain, wash thoroughly and put in a kettle of boiling water and boil until tender. Remove from water and take off outside skin. Stick with cloves and bake one hour in a slow oven.

Braised Heart

Cook as a pot roast or as follows:

Clean and wipe heart, cover with boiling water, steam two

hours; stuff with seasoned and moistened bread crumbs; place in baking dish, surround with brown gravy, cover dish closely and bake one hour.

Corned Beef Hash

½ small can corned beef.	1 small onion.
3 medium-sized cold-boiled potatoes.	Salt and pepper.

Chop meat, potatoes and onion in chopping bowl. Place in well-greased frying pan, add three or four tablespoons water and cook for five minutes with a cover. Remove cover and brown.

Cottage Pie

Cover the bottom of a greased baking dish with mashed potato, add cold meat (left-overs), salt, pepper and a few drops of onion juice. Cover with brown gravy and a layer of mashed potato and bake in oven until nicely browned.

Creamed Veal

1 cup cold veal cut in pieces.	1 cup white sauce (page 32).

Flank Steak

Remove skin from flank steak, stuff with nicely seasoned, moistened crumbs, roll, tie and bake.

Irish Stew

½ pound rump beef. Cut in pieces.	1 cup turnips.
½ pound breast lamb.	4 onions.
1 cup carrots.	2 potatoes.
	1 teaspoon salt.

Place meat in boiling water and cook slowly over low fire. When meat is half cooked add vegetables and boil until all are cooked. Remove meat and vegetables on a platter and thicken three cups of the water with two tablespoons of flour rubbed smooth in a little cold water. Pour over meat and vegetables.

Fricassée of Lamb

Use one pound of lamb cut from the shoulder and cut up in pieces for serving. Wipe meat, dredge with flour and brown quickly in frying pan with a very little fat. Remove to kettle and add just enough boiling water to cover meat, rinsing out frying pan. Cook until tender. For dumplings see baking powder biscuits (page 39). The dough is made soft, and dropped by spoonful on meat. Cover kettle tightly.

Broiled Bacon

Place thin slices of bacon on a wire broiler and bake in a hot oven over a dripping pan to save the fat, turning once. Drain. The fat then rendered out may be used for frying eggs, liver or in making gingerbread, etc.

Game

The flesh of game is usually very tender, is leaner than poultry but has a much stronger flavor. The meat is dark in color, except quail and partridge, and is cooked rare.

Pan Broiled Meat

Use one-half pound chopped meat for this—form into cakes, season, sear, cook in a sizzling hot greased frying pan, turning until brown on both sides. Serve with brown gravy. Do not allow any loose grease in the pan.

Brown Gravy

2 tablespoons melted fat (dripping).
2 tablespoons flour.
3 cups boiling water.

Brown fat, add flour, stir until smooth, add boiling water, season with salt, pepper and poultry seasoning.

Poultry

Poultry includes birds used for food, such as turkey, chicken, fowl, goose, duck.

To tell good poultry:

Clear skin.
Firm flesh.
If breast bone bends easily.
Eyes bright and full.

Broiled Chicken

Singe, wipe and cut a slit through backbone, the entire length of the bird, beginning at back of neck. Lay the bird open and remove organs. Cut out rib bones and remove from breast bone. Sprinkle with salt and pepper and place on a greased broiler and broil about fifteen minutes, turning often.

Fried Chicken

Cut chicken in pieces, wash and cook until tender in boiling salted water. Drain and place in well buttered frying pan and cook until well browned.

Roast Chicken or Turkey

Clean well, rub inside with salt, fill with stuffing, place in pan; after browning begins add cup of water and baste frequently.

Gravy

Chop giblets, cook until tender, pour off half of fat in pan; to remainder add enough flour to make a smooth paste, brown and add boiling water to make a smooth gravy. Add giblets.

Stuffing

Proportions.
1 cup crumbs.
⅓ cup butter (melted).
⅓ cup boiling water.
Powdered herbs, sage, summer savory or marjoram.

Pot Pies

Put chicken or lamb or beef stew in pudding dish, cover with baking powder crust (page 39) and bake.

Roast Beef

Place meat prepared for roasting in a dripping pan, skin side down and put in a hot oven to sear the surface, thus preventing the juice from escaping. If the meat is lean a piece of fat should be placed in the bottom of pan. Baste frequently, and when meat is half cooked turn so as to brown the other side.

Savory Sausages (*Chafing Dish*)

One dozen small steamed sausages. Prick skins and simmer in boiling water ten minutes. Melt two tablespoons butter in blazer. Cook sausages five minutes (turn). Add teaspoonful onion, one-quarter to one-half cup finely chopped celery, one-quarter to one-half cup tomato catsup. Let all heat and serve on toast.

Scalloped Rice and Meat

1 cup cooked rice.
½ pound chopped meat.
1 slice onion.

Line a greased baking dish with rice and cover with chopped meat well seasoned. Add another layer of rice and moisten with brown gravy or strained tomato juice. Brown in oven.

Tripe

Cut tripe in small pieces and stir into thin white sauce. Stew very gently for twenty minutes and season with lemon juice and minced parsley. For each pint stir in the beaten yolks of two eggs. This last should be done very quickly.

Veal Cutlets

Select veal cut about one-half inch in thickness from the leg. Cut in pieces for serving and dip each piece in flour, beaten egg and bread crumbs. Cook very slowly in well-greased frying pan with a cover. Veal requires a long, slow cooking to make it appetizing.

Reheated Tripe

½ pound cooked tripe.
2 tablespoons melted drippings.
½ small onion.
1 tablespoon vinegar.
Salt and pepper.

Cut up tripe, brown onion in dripping, add tripe, vinegar, salt and pepper. Heat thoroughly and serve with stewed tomato.

Broiled Hamburg Steak

Many do not realize that this can be cooked on a wire broiler. Make into oval cake, lay carefully on well-oiled broiler, cook over hot fire, and slip carefully on hot platter.

Stewed with Border of Pink Rice

Make an ordinary beef or lamb stew, place on platter, and surround with border of rice that has been cooked in strained stewed tomato juice. This gives an attractive pink color.

Boiled Tongue

Cook the same as boiled ham.

Veal Loaf

4 pounds veal.
¾ pound salt pork.
2 eggs.
Salt and pepper.

Chop meat, add eggs and seasoning and cook in greased bread pan with a little water.

CHAPTER XX

MILK

Modern science is throwing light on much that has been taken for granted until the present time. For generations milk has been accepted as a food for children and invalids, but it was left for the last decade to unfold the possibilities of this subject. Milk is now discussed in relation to its food value, its care "from cow to consumer," the dangers that may lurk in unclean milk, etc., etc.

The United States Government issues bulletins on milk, eminent physicians argue the question "To pasteurize or not to pasteurize," food specialists find new uses for it in making up dietaries, and so it goes.

Here follow some simple rules as to care and use of milk, with recipes for its preparation:

Care

Buy only bottled milk from a well-known firm. "Loose milk" is very unsafe.

Keep bottles in cool place.

Cleanse bottles as soon as emptied.

Keep milk covered, no matter where it stands.

Never allow anyone to drink from bottle or pitcher.

Keep certain dishes or pails for milk only, never put any other food in them.

Recipe for Junket

Dissolve one tablet in teaspoon of cold water. Heat one quart milk to blood heat, add three tablespoons sugar, one teaspoon vanilla and the dissolved tablet. Pour into cups and let stand undisturbed for half an hour.

CHAPTER XXI

NUTS

Nuts are a very nourishing food, and like cheese contain a large amount of nutriment in small space. Because of this fact it is unwise to eat nuts at the close of a hearty meal. A better plan is to have them prepared in such a manner that they can be easily masticated and then to use them as the chief dish of a meal.

Peanuts are the only nuts that are cheap, although almonds may be afforded occasionally. Both of these nuts should be made into meal, and then used in soup, or made into small cakes and cooked in the oven.

Chestnuts are also good to use in soups or croquettes.

Vegetarians depend very largely on nuts to take the place of meat, and in diabetes they are useful as a substitute for bread.

In all cases the pulverizing is necessary, otherwise nuts are difficult of digestion.

Nut butter makes a pleasant addition to the diet and may take the place of other butter.

The addition of nuts to cake and candy renders these foods more nutritive, although in this form they should be used sparingly.

Chestnut Soup

3 cups milk.
1 cup boiled and mashed chestnuts.
½ slice onion.
2 tablespoons butterine.
2 tablespoons flour.
Salt, pepper.

Cook nuts with stock and milk, season and bind with flour and butterine, smoothly blended.

Nut Bread

3½ cups pastry flour.
4 teaspoons baking powder.
½ to 1 cup sugar.
1½ cup milk.
¼ pound nuts.

Mix all together and bake in bread pan for one hour in a slow oven.

Nut Cookies

Yolks—2 eggs.
1 cup brown sugar.
1 cup chopped nut meats.
2 egg-whites.
6 tablespoons flour.
Few grains salt.

Beat yolks of eggs till thick, add sugar gradually, nut meats, whites of eggs beaten until stiff, flour and salt. Drop from tip of spoon on a greased tin. Spread and bake in a moderate oven.

Nut Salad

Mix chopped English walnuts with French dressing and serve on leaves of heart lettuce.

Nut Meal

This may be used for croquettes, sandwiches, cream soups or wafers. These latter are very useful in certain diseases, such as diabetes.

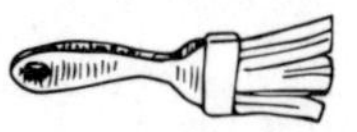 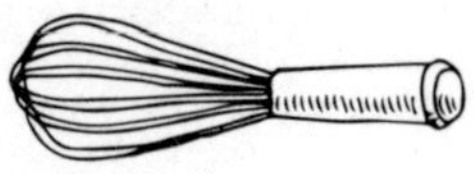

CHAPTER XXII

PIES

Crust for Two Pies

3 cups pastry flour.
1 teaspoon salt.
1 cup lard.

Cold water to make a dough.

Method

Rub or chop lard into sifted flour and salt, stir water in gradually, turn on floured board and roll out with quick, short strokes, folding and rolling three times. Line pie tins, put in filling and roll out upper crust, making slits in middle for steam to escape.

FILLINGS

Apple Pie

Pared sliced apples, sprinkled with sugar and spice, nutmeg or cinnamon.

Berry Pies

Sweetened berries, cooked with little or no water (if juicy), are used as fillings for pies.

Custard Pie

Custard (page 95) strained into one crust and baked. In each pie use two eggs and one and one-half cup milk, sweetened and flavored.

Lemon Pie

A soft cornstarch custard.

2 eggs.
1 cup boiling water.
1 cup sugar.
3 tablespoons cornstarch.
4 tablespoons cold water.
4 tablespoons lemon juice.
Grated rind of 1 lemon.
1 teaspoon butter.

Bake under crust, fill in custard (p. 97), cover top with the stiffly beaten whites of the eggs sweetened with two tablespoons powdered sugar. Brown slightly in oven.

Squash and Pumpkin Pies

In each pie use one and one-half cup strained squash or pumpkin, sweetened, flavored with ginger (one-fourth teaspoon) and mixed with one egg. Bake in one crust.

Rhubarb Pies

Cut up and sweeten rhubarb, without water, as it is very juicy. For one pie use two cups rhubarb, one cup sugar, one egg, two teaspoons butterine.

Mince Meat

To each cup of chopped cooked meat add two cups chopped apple, one cup brown sugar, one cup raisins. Add one teaspoon salt, one of cinnamon and one of allspice and one-half cup of water and one-fourth cup of lemon juice.

Cream Pie

Bake an under crust and fill with a sweetened and flavored cornstarch pudding. Brown in oven.

Prune Pies

Bake an under crust, fill with strained, stewed prunes, make cross strips of paste and bake. Make prune mixture rather thick.

Chocolate Pie

Make the same as cream pies, only flavor with chocolate before filling in the crust.

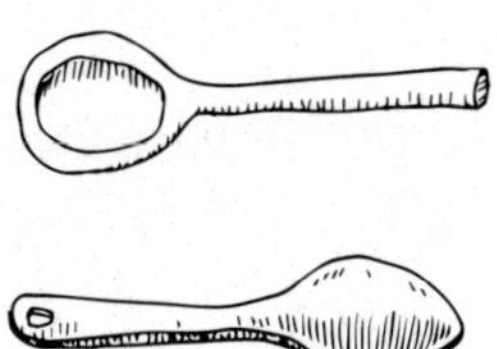

CHAPTER XXIII

PUDDINGS AND SAUCES

Apple Pudding

When apples are cheap, an excellent pudding may be made as follows:

5 apples.	1½ cup crumbs.

Grease a pudding dish, cover bottom of dish with stale bread crumbs, add a layer of sliced apples, sprinkle with sugar and cinnamon, then add another layer of crumbs, then apple, until dish is full; pour enough milk through the pudding to moisten it, before putting on top layer of crumbs; place four or five dots of butter on top. Cover pudding with a plate, bake until apples are tender, then remove plate and brown crumbs.

Apple Tapioca

6 tablespoons pearl tapioca.	¼ cup sugar.
Cold water to cover.	3 sour apples.
1¼ cup boiling water.	Speck salt.

Soak tapioca at least one hour in enough cold water to cover. Drain, add water and salt, and cook over hot water until transparent. Grease a baking dish and put in apples cut in small pieces. Cover with sugar and tapioca and bake in moderate oven till apples are soft. This pudding may be served with sugar and cream or milk. Dried fruit may be used if well soaked.

Baked Custard

1 egg.	Speck of salt.
1 cup milk.	Few drops vanilla.
1 tablespoon sugar.	

Scald milk and add to egg slightly beaten and sugar. Butter individual custard cups or baking dish and place in pan of water in a moderate oven for one-half hour. Test by inserting silver knife blade, straight up and down. If knife comes out clean, custard is done.

Charlotte Russe

Whip one-half cup of thick cream, add one-half cup of sugar and one teaspoon of vanilla. Serve on slices of sponge cake. (See page 43.)

Chocolate Bread Pudding

1 cup stale bread crumbs.	3 tablespoons sugar.
1 pint scalded milk.	1 egg.
1 square of chocolate.	Speck salt.

Soak crumbs in scalded milk, melt chocolate and add other materials. Place in buttered baking dish and bake in a moderate oven for twenty-five minutes.

Chocolate Pudding

Melt one and one-half tablespoons cocoa, add sugar and one-third cup boiling water, stir into boiling pudding (cornstarch).

Sauce.—Scald one pint milk, add to one beaten egg, sweeten to taste, cook three minutes.

Cornstarch Pudding

1 pint scalded milk.	¼ teaspoon salt.
4 tablespoons cornstarch.	½ teaspoon vanilla or little grated nutmeg.
4 tablespoons sugar.	

Stir cornstarch in a little cold water, add to boiling milk, add sugar and salt, stir until thick and smooth, cook fifteen minutes over hot water, add flavoring, remove from fire.

Cottage Pudding

Use rule for Mechanics' Institute Cake (page 44) and serve with a liquid pudding sauce.

Pudding Sauce

½ cup water.
1½ cup sugar.
4 teaspoons butterine.
2 tablespoons lemon juice or
2 teaspoons vanilla.

Make a syrup of sugar and water, boil ten minutes, add butter and flavoring.

Date Whip

15 dates (steamed).
½ cup sugar.
¼ tablespoon lemon juice.
2 egg-whites.

Beat eggs till stiff and add chopped dates, sugar and lemon juice, folding them in carefully. Put in buttered baking dish and bake until well browned.

Fruit Pudding

½ cup milk.
½ cup New Orleans molasses.
½ cup fruit, chopped.
1½ cups flour.
1 teaspoon soda.
½ teaspoon salt.
1 egg.
4 tablespoons melted suet.

Steam two and one-half hours. Serve with cream or any kind of pudding sauce.

Meringue

1 egg-white.
1 tablespoon sugar.
⅛ teaspoon vanilla.

Beat white until stiff, add sugar. Put in spoonfuls on top of simmering water and let remain until when tested it will not stick to fingers. Place on top of custard.

Plain Boiled Custard

1⅓ cup scalded milk.
2 egg-yolks.
3 tablespoons sugar.
Few drops vanilla.

Beat egg slightly, add sugar and milk which has been scalded. Pour all into saucepan or top of double boiler and cook over hot water until mixture thickens. Add vanilla and cool. If it begins to curdle while cooking remove from fire, place in pan of cold water and beat with egg beater. This will make it smooth.

Rice Dessert

1 cup fruit: Oranges, or pineapple or grape fruit.
½ cup sugar.
1 cup cold boiled rice.
1 cup whipped cream.

Mix together just before serving. A cherry may be placed on top as a garnish.

Rice Pudding Without Eggs

Wash four tablespoons rice, stir into one quart milk, add four tablespoons sugar, one tablespoon butter, one-half teaspoon salt. Bake until thick and creamy, about three hours.

Rice with Sugar and Cinnamon

Plain boiled rice makes a good dessert sprinkled with granulated sugar, which has been mixed with ground cinnamon to suit the taste.

Pudding Sauce

2 tablespoons butter.
½ cup brown sugar.
2 tablespoons cream or milk.
½ teaspoon vanilla.

Cream butter in a small bowl. Add sugar very slowly, beating all the time. Then gradually beat in the cream or milk and vanilla.

Simple Puff Pudding

1 pint flour.
2 teaspoons baking powder.
1¼ cup milk (or water).

Grease cups and put tablespoon of mixture in, then one tablespoon fruit (raisins, currants, fresh cherries, etc.) and cover with tablespoon of mixture. Steam twenty minutes and serve with any sweet sauce—the following may be used:

½ cup sugar.
1 cup water.

Boil until a thin syrup and add nutmeg.

Gelatine Dishes

Use granulated gelatine and soak in cold water until dissolved. This rule applies to all gelatine dishes.

Lemon Jelly

2 tablespoons gelatine.
2½ cups boiling water.
1 cup sugar.
½ cup lemon juice.

Stir dissolved gelatine into boiling water, add sugar and fruit juice, strain and cool.

Other Jellies

Use the above as a guide and vary flavoring, using orange and other fruit juices for variety.

Jellied Walnuts

Make the lemon jelly mixture, omitting the lemon juice; pour half in shallow pan; stir in halves of English walnut meats, about an inch apart, after it has begun to be firm; then pour on rest of mixture. Serve with whipped cream.

Fruit Jelly

Prepare ordinary jelly, and when beginning to harden stir in any combination of fruits to suit taste—sliced bananas, shredded pineapple, etc. This is a good use for small quantities of left-over fruit.

CHAPTER XXIV

RELISHES

Pickling is a method of preserving by means of an acid liquor or salt.

End of Season Pickle

2 quarts green tomatoes.
1 quart red tomatoes.
2 bunches celery.
3 red peppers.
3 green peppers.
3 large onions.
1 small cabbage.
1 cucumber.

Chop all finely and add a half cup salt and let stand all night. Drain and add—

3 pints vinegar.
2 pounds brown sugar.
1 teaspoon mustard.
1 teaspoon pepper.

Cook one hour. Put in preserving jars and seal.

Pickled Onions

Use small white onions. Peel and cover with brine (one and one-half cups salt with two quarts water) for two days. Drain and cover with another brine (one and one-half cups salt to two quarts water); let stand another two days. Heat to boiling and boil three minutes. Drain, rinse and place in pint jars. In each pint jar place

1 slice lemon.
2 pieces red pepper.
1 tablespoon brown mustard seed.
1 tablespoon white mustard seed.
1 teaspoon white peppercorns.
Small piece of mace.
Small piece of bay leaf.
1/8 teaspoon celery seed.
2 teaspoons sugar.

Fill to top of jar with boiling vinegar. (White wine vinegar is the best.)

Sweet Cucumber Pickles

Cover cucumbers with salt brine (one and a half cups salt to two quarts water) and let stand three days. Heat to boiling each day. Drain and slice lengthwise. Mix one quart vinegar and one and a half pound sugar and boil ten minutes. Add cucumbers and cook from fifteen to twenty minutes. (The above amount of syrup will be enough for one dozen cucumbers.)

Tomato Catsup

1 peck ripe tomatoes.
3 cups vinegar.
2 cups sugar.
3 tablespoons salt.
¼ teaspoon Cayenne.
2 sticks cinnamon.
1 tablespoon allspice.
1 tablespoon whole cloves.
1 tablespoon mustard seed.
½ teaspoon white pepper.
2 medium-sized onions.

Wash tomatoes, cut in pieces and add sliced onions. Cook one hour. Rub through sieve and place in kettle with remaining materials and cook until desired thickness. Strain and fill bottles. Cork tightly and seal with wax. The above amount will fill four bottles.

Tomato Relish

2 quarts tomatoes.
½ cup raisins.
2 pounds sugar.
2 lemons.
1 orange.

Peel tomatoes, slice orange and lemon, after washing well. Cook all materials together and simmer until thick.

Little Pickles

4 cups small cucumbers.
8 tablespoons salt dissolved in cold water.
2 red peppers.
1 tablespoon spice (mixed).
Boiling vinegar.

Scrub cucumbers, soak overnight in salt and water, drain, rinse, drain again, then place cucumbers with spice and peppers in jar, fill with boiling vinegar, cover, set in a cool place. When jar is opened replace vinegar with fresh, at boiling heat.

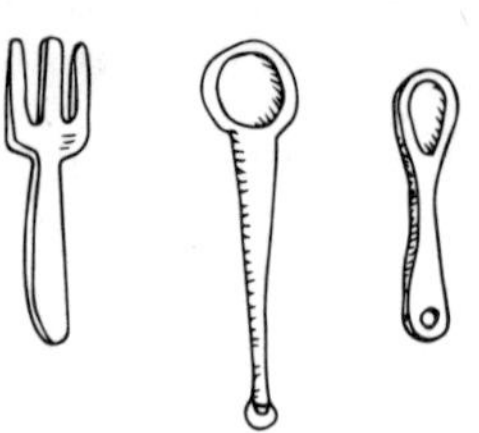

CHAPTER XXV

SALADS AND DRESSINGS

Most people do not realize the advantages of a salad as an every-day article of food. As a matter of fact, a salad should be an ordinary dish served as often as possible rather than an uncommon one.

A meat salad, such as chicken or veal, with a cooked or mayonnaise dressing, may form the main dish for a supper or luncheon, while for a dinner a simple vegetable salad, such as lettuce served with a French dressing, is more desirable.

Even in winter it is quite possible to serve salad, for our markets afford a large variety of greens, vegetables and fruits.

Salads should always be served cold. If the vegetables to be used are not strictly fresh, they may be made so by soaking in cold water. They should then be drained, dried and kept in a cool place until served. The dressing may be added at the table or just before bringing on.

Fruit Salad

Almost any combination of fruits may be used to make a fruit salad. Fruit should be cut with a silver knife.

To prepare oranges or grapefruit, remove peel and white covering, slice lengthwise that the tough center may not be sliced.

Bananas must be scraped to get rid of long threads inside of skin.

For each person—

1 lettuce leaf.
1 slice canned peach.
1 slice canned pear.
1 slice orange.
1 slice grapefruit.

Arrange fruit across lettuce leaf so that the deeper colored fruits will alternate with the lighter colored. Cover with a French dressing. This salad may be garnished with strips of red and green pepper laid on fruit.

Chicken Salad

Use twice as much cold cooked chicken as chopped celery. Mix together and add either mayonnaise or boiled dressing. Arrange on lettuce leaves and place a stuffed lime in the center of each portion.

Potato Salad

2 cups of cold potatoes (boiled or baked) cut in pieces.
1 small onion sliced.
1 small cucumber sliced.
Cooked salad dressing.

Serve on lettuce leaves and put radishes cut in pieces on top.

Cooked Dressing for above

1 tablespoon butterine.
1 tablespoon flour.
1 cup milk.
1 egg-yolk.
4 tablespoons vinegar.
1 teaspoon mustard.
1 teaspoon salt.
½ teaspoon sugar.
Few grains Cayenne pepper.

Melt butterine, add flour, stirring constantly. Remove from fire and add milk slowly. Cook until mixture boils. Add egg-yolk beaten slightly and cook over hot water two minutes. Remove from fire, place in pan of cold water and add vinegar and seasonings. This dressing may be put in a glass jar and will keep for several days.

French Dressing

1 tablespoon vinegar.
2 tablespoons olive oil.
¼ teaspoon salt.
Few grains pepper.
Few drops of lemon juice (if desired).

Mix materials together by vigorous beating.

Lobster Salad

Cut lobster meat in small pieces and cover with French dressing. Add an equal quantity of crisp, chopped celery, thoroughly drained, and place on lettuce leaves. Cover with mayonnaise dressing.

Macedoine Salad

½ cup cold boiled potatoes.
½ cup cold boiled carrots.
½ cup cold boiled peas.
½ cup cold boiled turnips.

Pour French dressing over vegetables.

Line a small salad bowl with lettuce leaves. Arrange vegetables in four sections in bowl.

Mayonnaise Dressing

1 egg-yolk.
½ teaspoon mustard.
½ teaspoon sugar.
½ teaspoon salt.
Few grains Cayenne pepper.
2 tablespoons vinegar.
2 tablespoons lemon juice.
1 cup olive oil.

Put egg in a bowl, add seasonings, vinegar and lemon juice. Beat all together with egg-beater or fork. Add oil by the teaspoon, beating mixture constantly until thick.

Pear Salad

Two large pears cut in small pieces, one small onion, a little chopped parsley, chopped walnuts, if desired. Use mayonnaise or French dressing, and, in either case, a little rich cream is a decided improvement. Serve on lettuce leaves.

Salmon Salad

1 small can of salmon.
¼ cup finely chopped celery.
Lettuce.
½ cup cooked salad dressing.

Drain salmon, remove bone and skin and pick into small pieces. Add celery and dressing and place on lettuce leaves.

Stuffed Tomato Salad

Wash two ripe tomatoes, cut off a slice from top of each and scoop out middle to form a cup, fill with chicken or celery salad, place cover on top, and serve on lettuce with mayonnaise dressing.

Banana Salad

Make a syrup by dissolving sufficient sugar to suit taste in the juice of half a lemon.

Cut up two bananas (one if salad is part of a meal) and pour syrup over. Cover and let stand an hour.

A Few Combinations

1. Lettuce and watercress—French dressing.
2. Lettuce and sliced onion—French dressing.
3. Lettuce, tomatoes halved and parsley—mayonnaise.
4. Lettuce, cold potatoes, beets—French dressing.
5. Lettuce and string beans—French dressing.
6. Lettuce, Neufchâtel cheese, olives—French dressing.
7. Lettuce and whole tomatoes stuffed with chopped cucumber and onion mixed with cooked dressing or mayonnaise.
8. Lettuce and hard cooked egg—cooked dressing.
9. Lettuce, grapefruit, celery, apple—mayonnaise dressing.
10. Shredded cabbage—pimento—cooked dressing.

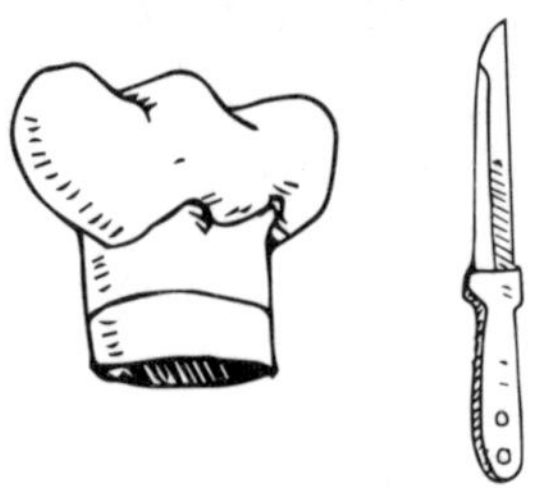

CHAPTER XXVI

SANDWICHES

For some time after their use began, sandwiches were very simple affairs, consisting of two slices of bread with a slice of meat between. It was easy to see that much could be done to make sandwiches both varied and attractive.

GENERAL RULES

Use bread one day old.

Cut bread very thin.

Cream butter with a spoon before spreading.

If cold meat is used, trim away all gristle and most of the fat.

Slice meat thin.

If lettuce is used, see that it is young and crisp.

Meats Good for Sandwiches

Cold corned beef dotted with mustard.

Cold chicken.

Cold boiled ham.

Cold roast beef.

Cold beefsteak, minced and seasoned with celery salt or Worcestershire sauce.

Cold tongue.

Other Attractive Sandwiches

Chicken salad sandwich. (See page 105.)

Cold boiled egg, chopped and mixed with salad dressing.

Peanut butter.
Chopped olives.
Chopped walnuts mixed with cream cheese.
Sliced Swiss or American cheese.

Club Sandwich

Toast two slices of bread. The filling should be first a thin slice of cold chicken, then a crisp lettuce leaf moistened with salad dressing, then another slice of chicken and two bits of bacon. Serve very hot.

Great variety of sandwiches may be made to suit individual taste, and anything that is appetizing may be used.

Boston Brown Bread Sandwiches

Slice Boston brown bread thin and serve with a filling of cream cheese.

To Cream Butter

Butter will spread much better if it is creamed in a bowl with the back of a spoon. It may then be flavored with lemon juice or anything desired.

Plain Lettuce Sandwiches

Slice Graham bread thin, wash tender lettuce, dry on towel, place between bread and butter after seasoning with salad dressing. Mayonnaise is best for this. See page 104.

CHAPTER XXVII

SOUPS

Meat Soups

Stock.—This is the foundation of all meat soups, and is made as follows:

One pound and a half shin of beef. Cold water to cover (about three cups). Wipe meat with damp cloth, cut in pieces, brown part of meat in frying pan with a little suet. Place all meat in kettle with water, add one-fourth teaspoon salt and simmer for three hours.

During last hour of cooking, add one small onion, one sprig of parsley and one-half bay leaf.

Strain stock and cool; skim off all fat. If a clear stock is desired, place the skimmed stock in saucepan, add one-half an egg-white and half a shell broken. Boil three minutes and simmer fifteen, then strain.

This skimmed and cleared stock is ready to be reheated and served plain with salt or with minced, cooked vegetables added, such as carrots, or cabbage, celery or canned peas, the amount to suit the taste.

Fish Stock

Select all parts of fish that are not edible—head, etc.—clean and cover with cold water, season and cook until bones separate from flesh. This may be the foundation of cream of fish. Thicken with flour and butter, season with onion, chopped parsley or anything preferred.

Mutton, lamb or chicken broth are simply stock made from these meats, served clear and seasoned with salt and pepper.

Additions

Barley is often added to beef broth. Rice to chicken and mutton broth, or to chicken soup.

Seasoning

One secret of appetizing soup is careful seasoning. The successful cook must be willing to taste and taste and taste again, and while it is good to follow exact rules in some cooking processes, in the matter of seasonings there is an opportunity to put real individuality into food by painstaking judgment.

The Stock Pot

The French have a trick of keeping a stock pot always on the stove, and of putting into this a few tablespoons of left over vegetables, or cereal, bits of toasted bread, and any savory food that will lend itself. This is an economical habit, and the American housekeeper would do well to adopt it, always supposing that she is willing to adopt also the careful French trait of extreme attention to detail, so that everything is exquisitely fresh and dainty, otherwise the stock pot may be both unattractive and a menace to health.

Oyster Soup

½ pint oysters. 2 cups thin white sauce (page 32).

Rinse oysters in cold water, remove all bits of shell. Parboil in oyster liquor and add oysters and liquor to hot white sauce.

Oyster Stew

The same as above, only that milk is unthickened and a little melted butter added.

Ox-Tail Soup

Cut ox-tail at the joints, brown in dripping, place in kettle with two quarts of cold water and a sliced onion and carrot, which have also been browned in the dripping; boil three hours, strain and bind with flour.

SOUPS WITHOUT STOCK OR MILK

Black Bean Soup

Make the same as lentil and split pea soup, and when done add four very thin slices of lemon and the chopped yolk of a hard boiled egg.

Hit-and-Miss Soup

1 cup of water drained from macaroni.
1 cup drained from cabbage.
2 small bones from roast veal.
1 scant tablespoon boiled rice.
1 tablespoon flour.

Simmer all together, thicken with the flour rubbed smooth in a little cold water.

Oatmeal Soup

½ cup oatmeal.
3 cups boiling water.
1 sprig celery.
Scalded milk.
½ teaspoon salt.
1 small onion.
1 teaspoon chopped parsley.

Cook oatmeal, salt, onion and celery together according to directions for cooking cereals, strain, add sufficient scalded milk to make soup as thin as desired (about one cup); add parsley just before serving.

Parsnip Soup

1 cup diced parsnips.
1 large potato or two small.
3 cups water.
Salt.
1 teaspoon butter.

Cook vegetables very soft, mash through strainer, add butter and seasoning.

Pea and Tomato Soup

1 cup shelled peas.
3 cups water.
1 slice onion.
1 tablespoon dripping.
Salt and pepper.
1 cup stewed, strained tomatoes.

Cook peas and onion in boiling water until very soft, strain, season, add melted fat and tomatoes.

Potato Soup

2 large potatoes.
1 pint water.
1 slice onion.
¾ teaspoon salt.
Pepper.
1 teaspoon chopped parsley.
2 tablespoons melted suet.
1 tablespoon flour.

Pare potatoes, cook in salted water, cut in cubes. Reserve water in which potatoes have been cooked for foundation of soup. Chop onion and brown in the fat, add flour, stir this into boiling soup, add potatoes and parsley, season and serve.

Split Pea Soup

½ cup split peas.
3 cups cold water.
1 slice onion.
½ tablespoon melted fat.
½ tablespoon flour.
¼ teaspoon salt.
Pepper to taste.

Wash peas, soak overnight, drain, add cold water and onion. Simmer three or four hours or until tender. Mash through strainer, bind with flour and fat cooked together.

Lentil Soup

Make the same as split pea soup.

Tomato Soup

½ can tomatoes.
1 cup water.
6 peppercorns.
Small bit of bay leaf.
1 small slice of onion.
1 teaspoon sugar.
½ teaspoon salt.
Speck of soda.
1 teaspoon melted dripping.
1½ teaspoon flour.

Cook tomatoes, water and seasoning for twenty minutes, strain, add soda, then bind with flour and fat cooked together.

Vegetable Soup

1 onion—chopped.
1 cup potato, cut in dice.
½ cup of carrot, diced.
½ cup of celery, sliced.
¼ cup beef dripping.
1 tablespoon flour.
4 cups water.
Salt and pepper.

Melt dripping, cook all vegetables except potato in this for ten minutes; add flour, parboil potato cubes and add to other vegetables; cook in the water one hour; season to taste.

CREAM SOUPS

Cream of Celery Soup

3 cups celery cut in bits.
2 cups boiling water.
2 cups milk.
3 tablespoons parsley.
½ slice onion.
2 tablespoons butter.
3 tablespoons flour.
Seasoning.

Wash and scrape celery, cut in pieces, cook in boiling water until very soft, mash through strainer, add milk which has been scalded with onion, bind with butter and flour cooked smooth, strain and add three tablespoons chopped parsley; season.

Cream of Corn Soup

½ cup corn.
1 cup water, boiling.
1 cup milk.
½ slice onion.
1 tablespoon butterine.
1 tablespoon flour.
½ teaspoon salt.
Pepper.

Chop corn, cook in water for fifteen minutes, strain, flavor milk by simmering with onion, make white sauce and add to corn.

Cream of Onion Soup

2 large onions.
1 cup milk.
½ tablespoon flour.
½ tablespoon butter.

Peel and slice onions, cook until very soft; mash through strainer, add half cup milk and heat again. Melt butter, add flour, stir into water in which onion was cooked (see that this boils before adding), pour into soup, add remaining milk and season.

Cream of Pea Soup

2 cups peas, canned or fresh.
1 cup water.
¼ teaspoon sugar.
1 cup thin white sauce (page 32).
¼ teaspoon salt.

Cook peas with sugar and water until very soft; mash through strainer with water, add to white sauce, season, and if too thick add more hot milk.

Cream of Potato Soup

½ cup mashed potato.
1 cup hot milk.
1 slice onion.
½ cup white sauce.
2 teaspoons chopped parsley.
Salt and pepper.

Cook onion and milk for ten minutes, remove onion, and stir flavored milk into mashed potato; add white sauce, strain, add more milk if needed, then parsley and serve.

Cream of Tomato Soup

1 cup stewed and strained tomato.
2 cups of thin white sauce (page 32).
⅛ teaspoon soda.

Make white sauce in usual way, and stir quickly into the strained tomato. Both sauce and tomato should be scalding hot when they are combined, and soup should be served at once to avoid curdling. More seasoning may be needed.

Cream of Asparagus

Boil the tough parts of stalks to make a " stock." Use one cup of this to each cup of white sauce (page 32).

Cream of Spinach

3 cups thin white sauce.
1 quart spinach.
1½ cups boiling water.
Salt and pepper.

Wash spinach, cook in boiling water with pinch of soda. Drain, chop, rub through colander. Add white sauce and reheat.

8

CHAPTER XXVIII

SPECIAL COOKING

For Infants, Children and Invalids

THE busy housewife often says, "I cannot prepare special food for anyone—all members of the family must fare alike." This is wise, if she means simply to discourage selfishness and "fussiness"; but there are times when some distinctions must be made.

The preparation of children's meals has already been spoken of (Chapter I, Part I) and this chapter will concern itself with the food of bottle-fed infants and with the food for sick persons.

The Food of Infants

If for any reason the mother cannot nurse the baby, the milk should be prepared very carefuly, and put in sterilized bottles.

If there are any signs of illness consult a physician. If the child is well the following tables will be helpful, although everything should be done by advice of the physician.

Modified Milk (Much Like Human Milk)

Top milk...........	8 ounces.	Lime water......	1 ounce.
Boiled water........	11 ounces.	Sugar of milk...	2½ tablespoons.

Food for Child—One Year to Eighteen Months

Breakfast.—Strained oatmeal with milk and small amount of sugar.

Lunch.—Zwieback and milk.

Dinner.—Soft cooked egg or broth with rice, junket or custard.

Supper.—Bread and milk.

Children from twenty to twenty-four months may add to the above bread and butter, baked potato, beef juice and stewed, strained fruit.

Cooking for Invalids

The choosing of food for the sick should be left to the physician or to some one who is competent to do this. In the preparation of the food, the same principles should be followed as in preparing food for the well (page 29).

A Few General Rules

Gruels.—These are prepared from any of the cereals in exactly the manner described in the preparation of breakfast cereal, the only difference being an increased proportion of water, the general proportion being about one part cereal to six of water.

Beef Juice

Broil a thick piece of round steak very lightly, and squeeze juice out with a lemon squeezer.

Beef Tea

Cut two pounds round steak very fine, removing all fat, place in Mason jar, screw on cover, place jar in kettle of cold water, place on stove, and bring slowly to boiling point. Cook until meat is gray, pour off juice, season and serve hot.

Scraped Beef

With a dull knife or spoon scrape the pulp of round steak free from the hard fiber. Spread raw in a sandwich, or make into small cakes and broil.

The preparation of eggs, soups, junket, broiled meat, cocoa and many other processes described in this book all furnish advices to those who have to cook for the sick. The keynote of invalids' food is simplicity, and hence the one in charge must learn the foundation principles of good cooking.

Brewis

1 cup Graham bread crumbs. Milk to cover.

Stir crumbs into milk and cook in oiled omelet pan until crumbs are soft. Season with salt.

Egg and Orange

Juice 1 orange. 1 egg.

Beat yolk of egg into orange juice, then fold in lightly the stiffly beaten white.

Egg Nog

1 tablespoon brandy.
2 teaspoons sugar.
⅔ cup milk.
Speck of salt.

Beat egg with brandy, sugar and salt, then stir in milk slowly.

Ice Cream for One

½ cup cream.
Speck of salt.
1 tablespoon sugar.
½ teaspoon vanilla.

Mix all together and freeze in small covered pail, set in larger pail. See page 79.

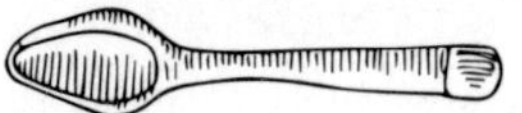

CHAPTER XXIX

VEGETABLES

Cooking of Vegetables

VEGETABLES should always be placed in boiling salted water and cooked until soft. If vegetables are cooked uncovered their color is kept better, and in the case of strong flavored vegetables, such as onions or cabbage, the odor will be less disagreeable in the house if cooked without a cover. If vegetables are soft or withered, they should be soaked in cold water for some time before cooking. They should always be thoroughly washed and scrubbed before cooking.

Dried vegetables should be soaked overnight if possible. This shortens the time needed for cooking.

Vegetables may be prepared in various ways, either raw as in salad or boiled and served with sauces combined with milk in making soups, steamed, baked or fried.

Spinach needs repeated washings, and if young and tender, can be cooked in its own juice, without water.

Carrots and Peas

1 cup carrots.
1 cup green peas.
1 tablespoon butter.

Wash, scrape and cut young carrots in small pieces and cook in boiling salted water until tender. Cook peas and add to carrots. Season with melted butter.

Corn Oysters

2 cups corn (removed from cob).
1 egg.
6 tablespoons flour.
½ teaspoon salt.
Few grains pepper.

Mix together and drop by spoonfuls on a hot greased griddle.

Eggplant

Pare, slice, soak overnight in cold water, dry between towels, dip in batter and fry in deep fat.

Fried Green Tomatoes

4 small green tomatoes.
1 small onion.
1 tablespoon drippings.

Remove skin from vegetables and cut in slices. Melt fat in frying pan and place vegetables in, cooking with a cover until they are soft.

Baked Potato

Wash four medium-sized potatoes. Place in a moderately hot oven and bake about forty minutes. If not served as soon as baked, they should be pierced with a fork to allow steam to escape so they will not become soggy.

Creamed Potatoes

2 cups cold boiled potatoes.
1 tablespoon butterine.
1 tablespoon flour.
1 cup milk.
½ teaspoon salt.

Melt butter, add flour, salt and milk, stirring constantly until mixture boils. Boil two or three minutes and add potatoes cut in pieces. Any vegetable may be used in this way.

Mashed Potatoes

6 medium-sized potatoes.
1 tablespoon butterine.
6 tablespoons hot milk.
½ teaspoon salt.
Few grains pepper.

Mash potatoes until all the lumps are out; add milk, butter, salt and pepper and beat with fork until light and flaky.

Scalloped Onions

Peel and boil one pint of onions; drain; add one cup of thin white sauce. Place in buttered baking dish and cover with two tablespoons buttered bread crumbs and bake on the grate of oven until brown.

Note.—Any vegetable may be used in place of the onions. Cabbage and potatoes are particularly good.

Steamed Squash

Cut winter squash in pieces and place in steamer for half an hour. Remove outside skin and pass pulp through a strainer. To one cup of squash add—

1 tablespoon butter.	Few grains pepper.
¼ teaspoon salt.	

Heat again and serve hot.

Stuffed Peppers

Remove stems and inside of green peppers, being careful not to cut the skin; place in boiling water and boil fifteen minutes; remove from water, drain and fill with stuffing made of chopped meat, moistened bread crumbs and seasoned with onion juice, salt and pepper. Bake until skins are tender, basting with water.

A Quick Way to Cream Vegetables

Cut cooked vegetables in dice, dredge with flour, stirring so that cubes are well covered; cover with milk, add a tiny bit of butter, season with salt and pepper, place on stove. When milk begins to cook stir vegetables until the milk is smooth and creamy.

BIBLIOGRAPHY

The following books will be found profitable reading for every housekeeper:

"The Home Science Cook Book," by Mary J. Lincoln and Anna Barrows. Whitcomb & Barrows, Boston. $1.00.

"The Feeding of Young Children," by Mary Swartz Rose. Teachers' College, Columbia University, New York City. $0.10.

"First Lessons in Food and Diet," by Ellen H. Richards. Whitcomb & Barrows, Boston. $0.30.

"Good Luncheons for Rural Schools," by Ellen H. Richards. $0.10.

"One Woman's Work for Farm Women," by Buell. Whitcomb & Barrows, Boston. Paper, 25 cents; postage, 5 cents.

"Care and Feeding of Children," by Emmet Holt, M.D. $0.75.

"Till the Doctor Comes and How to Help Him." Hope & Hydd. $1.00.

MENUS—ONE WEEK IN JANUARY

	SUNDAY	
BREAKFAST	DINNER	SUPPER
Oranges Cornmeal Pancakes Maple Syrup Coffee	Broiled Sirloin Steak Creamed Potatoes Broiled Onions Custard Coffee	Buttered Toast Apple Sauce Gingerbread Cheese Cocoa
	MONDAY	
BREAKFAST	LUNCHEON	DINNER
Stewed Prunes Shredded Wheat Milk and Sugar Creamed Codfish on Toast Coffee	Split Pea Soup, Croutons Lettuce with Mayonnaise Bread and Butter Cocoa or Tea with Tea Ball	Braiséd Shoulder Chops Baked Potatoes Peas Fruit Pudding Coffee
	TUESDAY	
Oatmeal with Bananas Milk and Sugar Toast Coffee	Cheese Fondu Stewed Fruit Cookies Tea	Baked Beans with Bacon Stewed Tomato Apple and Celery Salad Coffee
	WEDNESDAY	
Cornmeal Mush Syrup Broiled Hamburg Steak Toast Coffee	Kippered Herring Fried Mush Tea Drop Cakes Stewed Apricots	Shoulder of Mutton Baked Sweet Potatoes Cornstarch Pudding
	THURSDAY	
Corn Flakes Pan Fish Brown Potatoes Baking Powder Biscuit Coffee	Salmon Salad Bread and Butter Baked Apples Cocoa	Lentil Soup—Croutons Hamburg Roll Scalloped Cabbage Cream of Rice Coffee
	FRIDAY	
Wheatena with Dates Milk and Sugar Broiled Tripe Toast Coffee	Mock Bisque Rolls Cabbage Salad Cocoa	Boiled Cod, Egg Sauce Boiled Potatoes Scalloped Tomatoes Apple Dumpling Coffee
	SATURDAY	
Oranges Wheat Cakes Maple Syrup Coffee	Creamed Fish Scalloped or Baked Potatoes Gingerbread—Tea	Pork Tenderloin Potatoes, Brown Gravy Scalloped Onions Sliced Bananas Cream and Sugar

MENUS—ONE WEEK IN FEBRUARY

SUNDAY

BREAKFAST	DINNER	SUPPER
Popovers Scrambled Eggs Stewed Fruit Coffee	Chicken Fricassée with Biscuits Mashed Potatoes Boiled Onions Home-made Ice Cream Coffee	Cream Cheese Sandwiches Olives Sardines Canned Fruit Tea

MONDAY

BREAKFAST	LUNCHEON	DINNER
Vienna Rolls Orange Marmalade Minced Chicken Coffee	Clam Chowder Boston Crackers Apple Dumpling Tea	Baked Haddock Mashed Carrots Baked Potatoes Indian Pudding Coffee

TUESDAY

Cream of Wheat with Raisins Milk and Sugar Fruit Toast—Coffee	Ox-tail Soup Boiled Rice with Butter Ginger Cookies Tea	Pot Roast Mashed Potatoes Creamed Carrots Pumpkin Pie Coffee

WEDNESDAY

Oranges Popovers Hash Coffee	Fish Balls Brown Bread and Butter Cocoa	Beef Cutlets, Braiséd Rice and Butter Creamed Cabbage Apple Pie, Coffee

THURSDAY

Fried Bananas Toast Coffee	Pigs in Blankets Bread and Butter Stewed Fruit Tea	Corned Beef Cabbage Boiled Potatoes

FRIDAY

Oranges Creamed Finnan Haddie Rolls Coffee	Macedoine Salad Bread and Butter Oat Wafers Cheese Tea	Cream of Corn Corned Beef Hash Horseradish Parsnips Orange Jelly Coffee

SATURDAY

Oatmeal, Cream and Sugar Boiled Eggs Toast Coffee	Club Sandwich Cocoa	Beefsteak Pie Egg Plant Stewed Tomatoes Cottage Pudding

MENUS—ONE WEEK IN MARCH

SUNDAY

BREAKFAST	DINNER	SUPPER
Boston Baked Beans	Roast Leg of Mutton	Salmon Salad
Brown Bread	Mashed Potatoes	Peanut Butter Sandwiches
Coffee	Oyster Plant	Cocoa
	Coffee Jelly	
	Coffee	

MONDAY

BREAKFAST	LUNCHEON	DINNER
Shredded Wheat	Scalloped Oysters	Cold Roast Mutton
Date Marmalade	Bread and Butter	Currant Jelly
Minced Meat on Toast	Stewed Fruit	Lettuce Salad
	Tea	Potato Cakes
		Prune Whip
		Coffee

TUESDAY

Oatmeal	Tomato Soup	Lamb Pot Pie
Baked Apples	Hot Biscuits	Cabbage Salad
Toast	Tea	Fried Egg Plant
Coffee		Baked Bananas
		Coffee

WEDNESDAY

Fried Mush	Fried Oysters	Broiled Chops
Syrup	Rolls	Tomato Sauce
Poached Eggs	Tea	Creamed Potatoes
Coffee	Pickles	Tapioca Creamed
		Coffee

THURSDAY

Wheatena	Split Pea Soup	Beef en Casserole
Blatters	Cheese—Crackers	Baked Potatoes
Buttered Toast	Tea	Rice Pudding
Coffee		Coffee

FRIDAY

		Cream of Celery Soup
Cereal	Salmon Salad	Veal Cutlet
Creamed Codfish on Toast	Hard Rolls	Mashed Potatoes
Prunes	Fruit Cookies	Shredded Cabbage
Coffee	Cocoa	Steamed Pudding
		Coffee

SATURDAY

Hominy Croquettes	Lettuce Sandwiches with Mayonnaise	Slices of Fish
Kippered Herring	Canned Cherries	Creamed Potatoes
Baked Apples	Cake	String Beans
Coffee	Tea	Junket
		Coffee

MENUS—ONE WEEK IN APRIL

SUNDAY

BREAKFAST	DINNER	SUPPER
Grape-Nuts Salt Mackerel Hashed Brown Potatoes Toast Coffee	Veal Loaf Boiled Rice Spinach Chocolate Bread Pudding	Cream of Onions Nut Salad Baking Powder Biscuit Tea

MONDAY

BREAKFAST	LUNCHEON	DINNER
Milk Toast Scrambled Eggs Coffee	Club Sandwiches Cocoa	Beef Stew Potatoes Greens Canned Blueberry Pudding Coffee

TUESDAY

Wheatena Boiled Eggs Toast Coffee	Potato Salad Bread and Butter Sandwiches Olives Tea	Lamb Chops Asparagus Hominy Cream Cheese Wafers Coffee

WEDNESDAY

Boston Brown Bread Omelet Coffee	Cheese Pudding Tea	Lamb Pot Pie Pot Roast Parsnips Boiled Rice Sliced Bananas Coffee

THURSDAY

Oatmeal Creamed Codfish on Toast Coffee	Hash Creamed Asparagus Bread and Butter Tea	Lentil Soup Macaroni and Cheese Spinach Baked Custard Coffee

FRIDAY

Cornmeal Pancakes Brown Sugar Syrup Coffee	Scalloped Eggs Rolls Cookies—Jam Tea	Beef Stew Boiled Rice Pickles Dandelion Greens Cottage Pudding Coffee

SATURDAY

Buttered Toast Chipped Beef Coffee	Cream Tomato Soup Hot Biscuits Stewed Fruit Tea	Baked Hamburg Stewed Potatoes Shredded Cabbage Boiled Dressing Floating Island Coffee

MENUS—ONE WEEK IN MAY

SUNDAY

BREAKFAST	DINNER	SUPPER
Sliced Oranges	Broiled Steak	Salmon Loaf
Liver and Bacon	Mashed Potatoes	Lettuce Salad
Toast	Canned Tomato	Gingerbread
Coffee	Lemon Sherbet	Tea
	Wafers	
	Coffee	

MONDAY

BREAKFAST	LUNCHEON	DINNER
Pan Fish	Cheese Fondu	Minced Meat (from Steak)
Fried Potatoes	Tea	Scalloped Potatoes
Toast		Canned Corn
Coffee		Caramel Custard
		Coffee

TUESDAY

Wheatlet	Macaroni au Gratin	Veal Roast
Bacon and Eggs	Stewed Fruit	Spinach
Toast	Plain Cake	Potatoes
Coffee	Tea	Creamy Rice
		Coffee

WEDNESDAY

Eggs Poached in Milk	Cold Sliced Veal	Baked Beans
Toast	Pickles	Canned Tomato
Coffee	Brown Bread and Butter	Shredded Cabbage
	Tea	Prune Pudding
		Coffee

THURSDAY

Stewed Apricots	Club Sandwiches	Broiled Chops
Minced Meat (from Roast)	Cocoa	Canned Corn
Toast		Hominy
Coffee		Apple Pudding
		Coffee

FRIDAY

Cream of Wheat	Egg Salad	Broiled Fish
Stewed Raisins	Rolls	Potatoes
Johnnycake	Tea	Lettuce Salad
Coffee		Tarts with Filling of Canned Fruit

SATURDAY

Bacon	Corn Oysters	Fish Chowder
Potato Cakes	Rolls	Rice and Cheese
Fruit Toast	Stewed Prunes	Scalloped Tomato
Coffee	Cookies	Cream Pie
	Tea	Coffee

MENUS—ONE WEEK IN JUNE

SUNDAY

BREAKFAST

Stewed Prunes
Pop-overs
Broiled Tomatoes
Coffee

DINNER
Cream of Tomato Soup
Croutons
Breast of Veal
Brown Potatoes
Asparagus
Strawberry Short Cake

SUPPER
Tomato Salad with
Mayonnaise
Brown Bread and Butter
Sandwiches
Strawberries
Iced Tea

MONDAY

BREAKFAST

Vienna Rolls, Heated
Sliced Pineapple
Coffee

LUNCHEON
Sliced Tomatoes
French Dressing
Brown Bread and Butter
Tea

DINNER
Broiled Steak
Old Potatoes, Mashed
Asparagus
Strawberry Short Cake
Coffee

TUESDAY

Rice, Sugar and Cream
Buttered Toast
Strawberries
Coffee

Toasted Bread Crumbs
in Milk
Baked Cup Custard

Veal Chops, Braiséd
Green Peas
Mashed Potatoes
Strawberry Pie
Coffee

WEDNESDAY

Shredded Wheat
Omelet
Buttered Toast
Coffee

Muffins
Sliced Bananas
Cream and Sugar
Tea

Broiled Bluefish
Stewed Potatoes
Cucumbers, Sliced—
French Dressing
Strawberry Gelatine
Coffee

THURSDAY

Strawberries
French Toast
Bacon
Coffee

Cheese Sandwiches
Lettuce Salad
Iced Tea

Potato Soup
Hamburg Roll
Asparagus
Sliced Pineapple
Wafers
Coffee

FRIDAY

Poached Eggs
Frizzled Beef
Toast
Coffee

Banana Salad
Crisp Rolls
Coffee

Boiled Fish—
Egg Sauce
Stewed Tomatoes
Cornstarch—Custard
Coffee

SATURDAY

Wheatena
Broiled Bacon
Toast
Coffee

Minced Fish
Lettuce Sandwiches
Junket
Tea

Cream of Pea Soup
Bread Sticks
Beef Cutlets, Braiséd

MENUS—ONE WEEK IN JULY

SUNDAY

BREAKFAST
Small Fried Fish
Radishes
Rolls
Coffee

DINNER
Cream of Pea Soup
Broiled Chops
Creamed Potatoes
Blueberry Cake

SUPPER
Cheese Sandwiches
Boiled Ham
Cake
Tea

MONDAY

BREAKFAST
Cream of Wheat
Ham Omelet
Toast
Coffee

LUNCHEON
Potato Salad
Bread and Butter
Sandwiches
Iced Tea

DINNER
Lamb Fricassée
Potatoes
Cucumber Salad
Lemon Sherbet
Coffee

TUESDAY

Boiled Rice with Raisins
Milk and Sugar
Huckleberries
Toast
Coffee

Scalloped Eggs
Graham Muffins
Tea

Breast of Lamb
Green Peas
Brown Potatoes
Fruit Gelatine
Coffee

WEDNESDAY

Grape-Nuts
Minced Lamb on Toast
Coffee

Toasted Bread Crumbs in Milk
Sliced Bananas

Slice of Fish, Broiled
Potatoes in Milk
Asparagus
Tapioca, Creamed
Coffee

THURSDAY

Poached Eggs
Fried Mush, Brown Sugar
Syrup
Coffee

Cream Cheese Sandwiches
Blueberries
Milk

Stuffed Steak
String Beans
Boiled Rice
Sliced Pineapple and Bananas
Coffee

FRIDAY

Wheatena
Codfish Balls
Toast
Coffee

Cold Sliced Steak
Rolls
Coffee

Bluefish
Creamed Potatoes
Cucumber Salad
Philadelphia Ice Cream
Coffee

SATURDAY

Braiséd Liver
Toast
Coffee

Bread and Milk
Ginger Cookies

Celery Soup
Veal Cutlet
Browned Potatoes
Cheese
Wafers
Coffee

MENUS—ONE WEEK IN AUGUST

SUNDAY

BREAKFAST

Milk Toast
Stewed Berries
Coffee

DINNER
Roast Lamb
Potatoes
String Beans
Watermelon
Coffee

SUPPER
Egg Salad
Rolls
Raspberries
Milk

MONDAY

BREAKFAST

Broiled Mackerel
Sliced Tomatoes
Toast
Coffee

LUNCHEON

Corn Fritters
Stewed Fruit
Iced Tea

DINNER
Clam Chowder
Cold Lamb
Green Peas
Sliced Fruit with Whipped Cream
Coffee

TUESDAY

Rice and Milk
Boiled Eggs
Toast
Coffee

Canteloupe
Baking-powder Biscuits
Iced Tea

Bluefish
Sliced Tomatoes and Cucumbers
Boiled Rice with Butter
Sliced Peaches

WEDNESDAY

Shredded Wheat
Berries
Coffee

Creamed Codfish
Brown Bread and Butter
Iced Tea

Broiled Steak
Stuffed Tomatoes
Creamed Potatoes
Cheese
Wafers
Coffee

THURSDAY

Sliced Peaches
Buttered Toast
Coffee

Peanut Butter Sandwiches
Lettuce Salad
Cake
Tea

Lamb Pie
Boiled Rice or Hominy
Lima Beans
Sherbet
Coffee

FRIDAY

Muffins
Stewed Huckleberries
Coffee

Club Sandwiches
Peaches
Iced Tea

Salmon, Boiled
Creamed Potatoes
Peas
Chocolate Cornstarch
Coffee

SATURDAY

Rice Pancakes
Scrambled Eggs
Coffee

Brown Bread and Butter
Cold Bean Salad
Peaches and Teaspoon Milk
Iced Tea

Broiled Chicken
Potatoes
Tomato Salad
Caramel Ice Cream
Coffee

MENUS—ONE WEEK IN SEPTEMBER

SUNDAY

BREAKFAST	DINNER	SUPPER
Melon	Liver and Bacon	Beet Salad
Omelet	Creamed Onions	Rolls
Toast	Bread Pudding	Cake
Coffee	Coffee	Iced Tea

MONDAY

BREAKFAST	LUNCHEON	DINNER
Muffins	Huckleberries	Chicken en Casserole
Coffee	Bread and Butter	Boiled Rice
	Milk	Green Corn
	Ginger Cookies	Orange Ice
		Coffee

TUESDAY

Wheatena	Minced Chicken	Pea Soup
Milk and Sugar	Biscuits	Cheese Pudding
Bacon and Eggs	Tea	Onions
Coffee		Baked Custard
		Coffee

WEDNESDAY

Moulded Wheatena with Fruit	Corn Bread	Calves Liver
Codfish Hash	Blackberries	Corn on Cob
Toast	Milk	Baked Potatoes
Coffee		Tomato Salad
		Cheese
		Wafers
		Coffee

THURSDAY

Muskmelon	Stewed Pears	Veal Loaf
Fried Eggs	Biscuits	Potatoes
Toast	Tea	Buttered Beets
Coffee		Peaches and Cream
		Coffee

FRIDAY

Cream of Wheat	Corn Pudding	Fish en Casserole
Baked Bananas	Apple Salad	Scalloped Potatoes
Toast	Wafers	Tapioca Pudding
Coffee	Tea	Coffee

SATURDAY

Creamed Fish on Toast	Cheese Fondu	Beef Stew with Biscuit Crust
Coffee	Wafers	Lettuce Salad
	Tea	Ice Cream
		Coffee

MENUS—ONE WEEK IN OCTOBER

SUNDAY

BREAKFAST	DINNER	SUPPER
Graham Muffins Fish Cakes Coffee	Hamburg Steak Creamed Cauliflower Boiled Hominy Baked Custard Coffee	Brown Bread Smoked Halibut Cake Tea

MONDAY

BREAKFAST	LUNCHEON	DINNER
Grapes Wheat Cakes Omelet Coffee	Welsh Rarebit Cornstarch Custard Tea Wafers	Lamb Broth Boiled Rice Sweet Potatoes Apple Tapioca Coffee

TUESDAY

Wheatena with Raisins Baked Bananas Toast Coffee	Apple Sauce Brown Bread Poached Eggs Tea	Pork Chops Fried Apples Baked Potatoes Celery Lemon Jelly Coffee

WEDNESDAY

Poached Eggs Toast Fried Potatoes Coffee	Bread and Milk Ginger Cookies	Corned Beef Shredded Cabbage Boiled Potatoes Apple Pie Coffee

THURSDAY

Corned Beef Hash Toast Coffee	Egg Sandwiches Cocoa	Stock Soup Rice and Cheese Scalloped Onions Remainder of Pie Coffee

FRIDAY

Graham Muffins Grapes Scrambled Eggs Coffee	Fish Chowder Lettuce Sandwiches Tea	Celery Soup Braised Flank Sweet Potatoes Onions Prune Pudding Coffee

SATURDAY

Shirred Eggs Rolls Coffee	Cheese Toast Apple Sauce Tea	Breaded Chops Scalloped Potatoes Squash Fruit Pudding Coffee

MENUS—ONE WEEK IN NOVEMBER

SUNDAY

BREAKFAST	DINNER	SUPPER
Baked Apples	Roast Chicken	
Creamed Potatoes	Mashed Potatoes	Scalloped Oysters
Rolls	Creamed Onions	Rolls
Coffee	Rice Pudding	Chocolate
	Coffee	

MONDAY

BREAKFAST	LUNCHEON	DINNER
		Other Half of Chicken
Oatmeal	Cream of Corn (canned)	Potatoes
Bacon	Soup	Cauliflower
Rolls	Buttered Toast	Cheese
Coffee	Tea	Wafers
		Coffee

TUESDAY

Cornmeal		Meat en Casserole
Codfish Hash	Fried Mush	Baked Sweet Potatoes
Toast	Milk	Bread Pudding
Coffee		Coffee

WEDNESDAY

		Lentil Roast
Corn Dodgers	Cheese Fondu	Tomato Sauce
Bacon	Cocoa	Potatoes
Coffee		Lemon Jelly
		Coffee

THURSDAY

Oatmeal		Broiled Steak
Baked Apples	Sardines on Toast	Creamed Onions
Toast	Stewed Fruit	Mashed Turnip
Coffee	Cocoa	Cottage Pudding
		Coffee

FRIDAY

Fish Balls		Baked Beans
Brown Bread	Bread and Milk	Scalloped Tomatoes
Toast	Custard	Creamed Potatoes
Coffee		Junket
		Coffee

SATURDAY

Barley, Butter and Sugar	Baked Beans, Salad	Pork Chops
Kippered Herring	Rolls	Baked Potatoes
Toast	Stewed Fruit	Oyster Plant
Coffee	Coffee	Jellied Nuts
		Coffee

MENUS—ONE WEEK IN DECEMBER

SUNDAY

BREAKFAST	DINNER	SUPPER
Oranges Pancakes Sausages Coffee	Split Pea Soup Hamburg Roll Browned Potatoes Cheese Wafers Coffee	Salmon Salad Rolls Cocoa

MONDAY

BREAKFAST	LUNCHEON	DINNER
Cornmeal Bacon Toast Coffee	Rolls Poached Eggs Cocoa	Beefsteak Pie Stewed Celery Pumpkin Pie Coffee

TUESDAY

Fried Mush Syrup Bananas Coffee	Cheese Soup Croutons Apple Sauce Cocoa	Fried Oysters Celery Scalloped Tomato Squash Pie Coffee

WEDNESDAY

Creamed Finnan Haddie Toast Coffee	Cheese and Olive Sandwiches Stewed Apricots Wafers Cocoa	Chicken Fricassée Dumplings Onions Salad of Winter Vegetables Apple Pie Coffee

THURSDAY

Oatmeal Creamed Toast Coffee	Salmon Loaf Rolls Gingerbread Cocoa	Other Part of Chicken on Toast Baked Potatoes Sweet Potatoes Shredded Cabbage Junket Coffee

FRIDAY

Oatmeal Codfish Hash Toast Coffee	Wheat Cakes Maple Syrup Milk	Baked Fish Mashed Carrots Potatoes Prune Pie Coffee

SATURDAY

Shredded Wheat Stewed Prunes Coffee	Scalloped Eggs Rolls Coffee	Black Bean Soup Minced Fish in Cups Baked Potatoes Canned Tomatoes Steamed Pudding Coffee

PART III

GOVERNMENT BULLETINS

The U. S. Department of Agriculture, at Washington, D.C., issues a series of pamphlets, anyone of which may be procured by sending a postal card with the request for the pamphlets desired.

Address:

THE U. S. DEPARTMENT OF AGRICULTURE,
WASHINGTON, D.C.,

and order by numbers, as follows:

Farmers'	Bulletin,	No.	121	beans.
"	"	No.	112	bread.
"	"	No.	128	eggs.
"	"	No.	80	fish.
"	"	No.	391	meat.
"	"	No.	42	milk.
"	"	No.	332	nuts.
"	"	No.	93	sugar.
"	"	No.	256	vegetables.

The following food charts are prepared by Dr. C. F. Langworthy, of the Department of Agriculture, and a set for hanging can be procured for one dollar.

Definitions

Carbohydrates—Sugar and starches.
Calories—Unit used in calculating heat value.
Protein—Strength-giving substance.

COMPOSITION OF FOOD MATERIALS

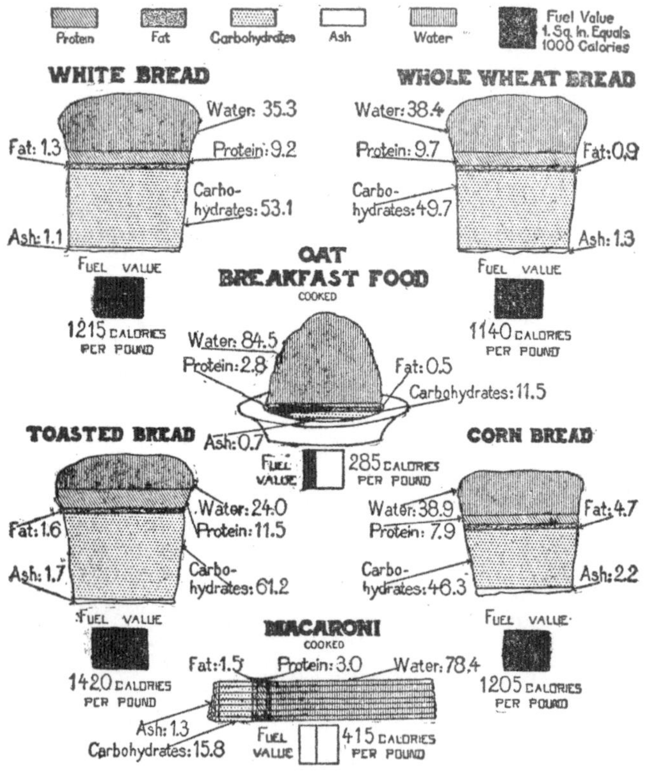

U.S. Department of Agriculture
Office of Experiment Stations
A C. True: Director

Prepared by
C. F. LANGWORTHY
Expert in Charge of Nutrition Investigations

These foods, bread, toast, macaroni, etc., give both heat and strength. It will be noticed that the only difference between bread and toast is in the amount of water. The protein spoken of stands simply for the strength-giving properties, the carbohydrate for the heat. The term calorie refers to the amount of energy given.

COMPOSITION OF FOOD MATERIALS

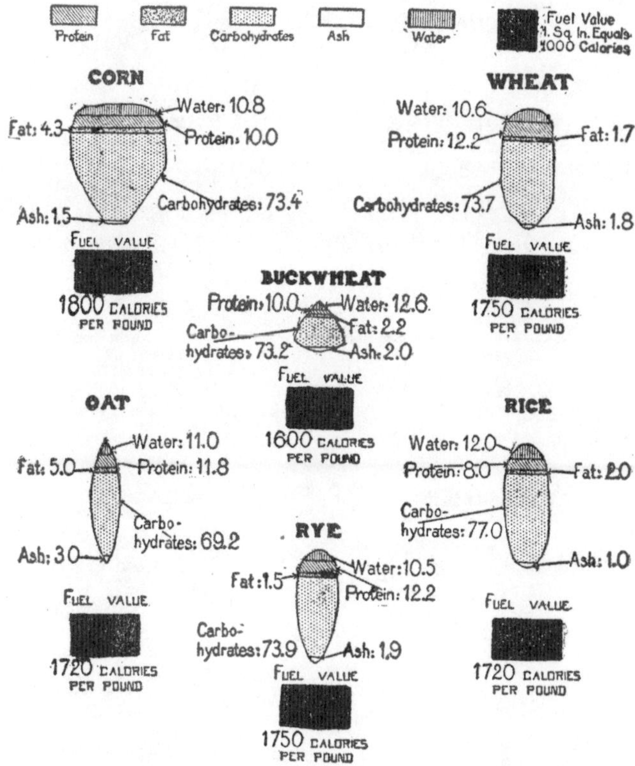

U.S. Department of Agriculture
Office of Experiment Stations
A.C. True: Director

Prepared by
C.F. LANGWORTHY
Expert in Charge of Nutrition Investigations

Wheat is the most useful of these, although corn has a higher heat value. Rice gives only heat and no strength, while rye is rather difficult of digestion.

COMPOSITION OF FOOD MATERIALS

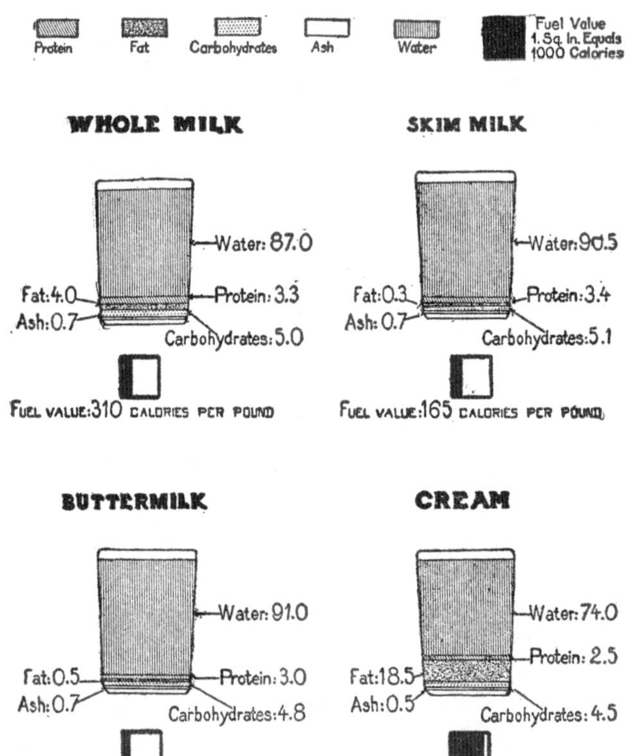

This also belongs to the strength group, and the cream has most fat, but the whole milk is most generally useful. Buttermilk is useful in the cases of disordered digestion.

COMPOSITION OF FOOD MATERIALS

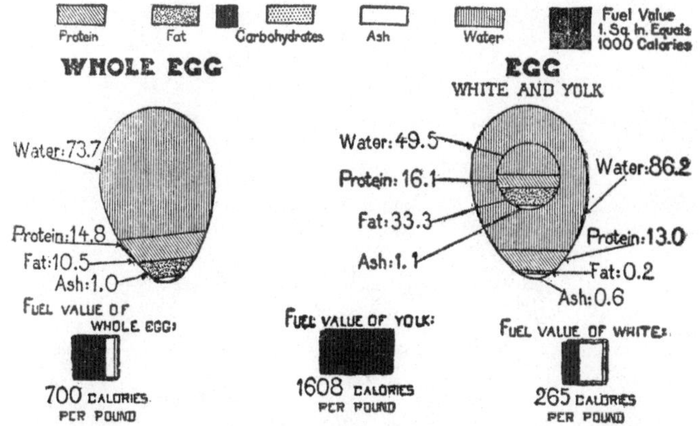

CREAM CHEESE

COTTAGE CHEESE

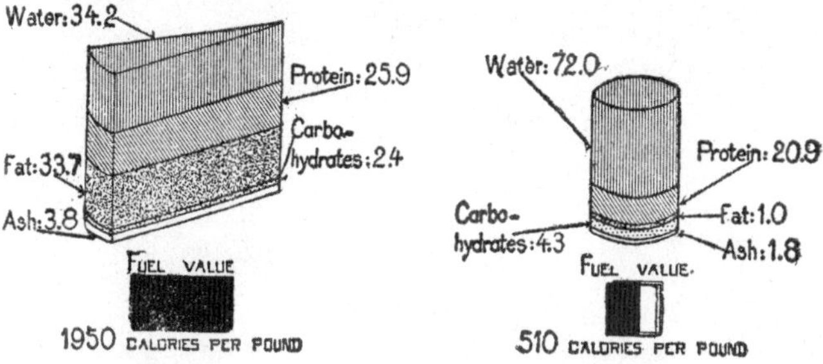

U.S. Department of Agriculture
Office of Experiment Stations
A.C. True: Director

Prepared by
C.F. LANGWORTHY
Expert in Charge of Nutrition Investigations

Both of these foods belong to the strength group, and the different varieties of cheese are a great help in adding strength to starchy food, although the kind known as American cheese will do this most economically.

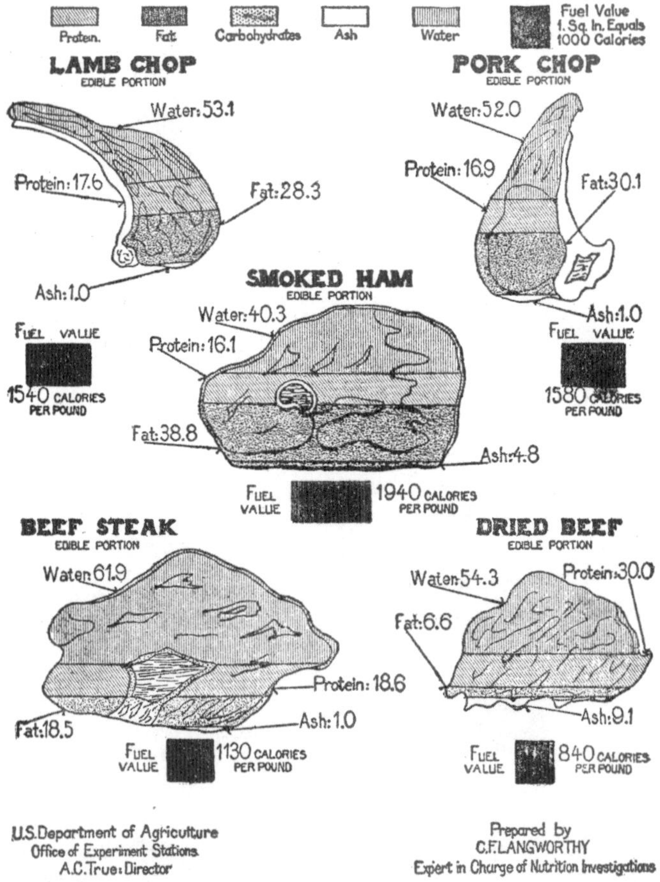

These are the strength foods. There is not much apparent difference between lamb and pork chops, although lamb is much more wholesome. The smoked ham is not a valuable food, as the smoking process takes away from the strength-giving qualities. Of these meats, steak is the most valuable.

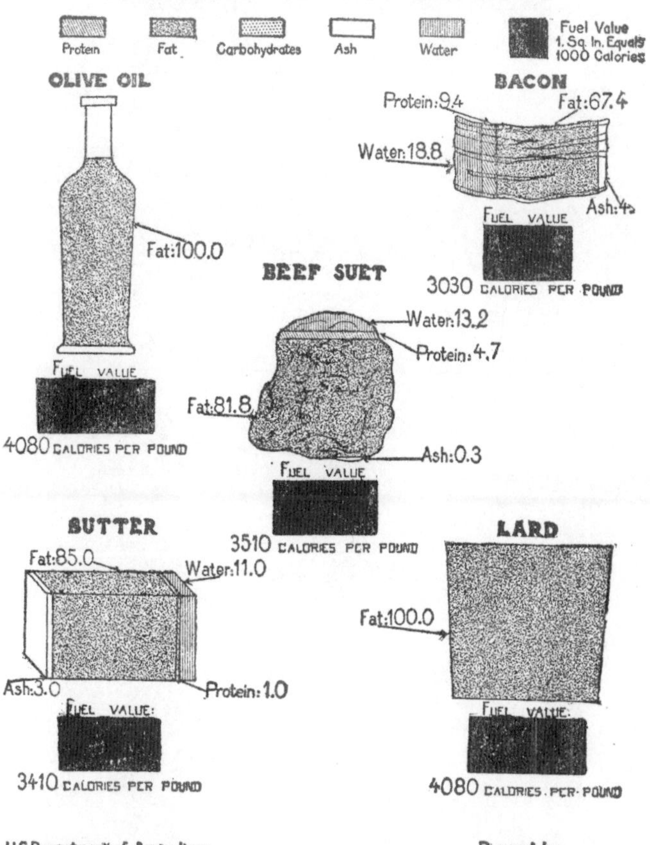

These foods are almost pure fat, and it will be seen that the caloric value is high, because fat gives a large amount of heat. Pure oil is one of the most wholesome of fats. The fat of bacon is also wholesome, and to use as shortening, beef suet is much better than lard, except in some cases where a soft fat is needed to give tenderness, as in the case of baking-powder biscuits and pastry.

COMPOSITION OF FOOD MATERIALS

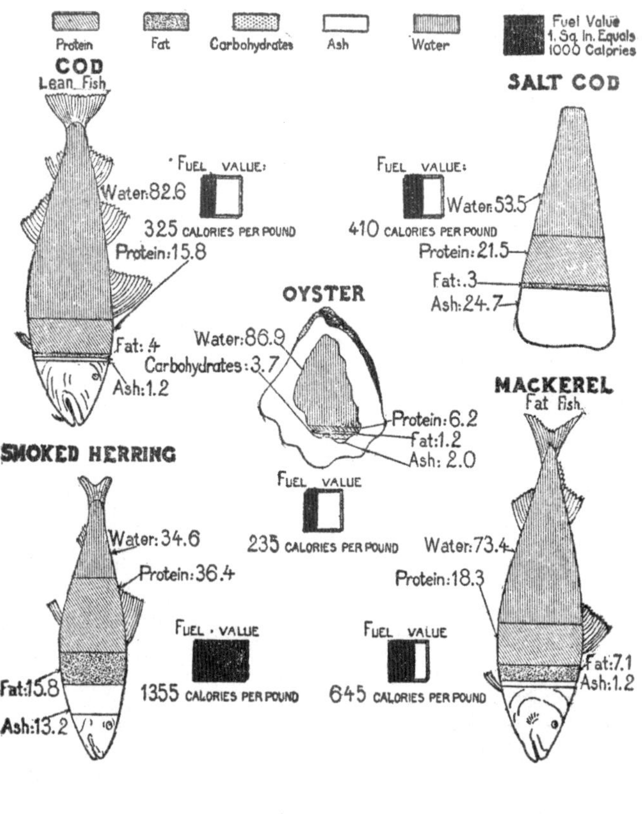

U.S. Department of Agriculture
Office of Experiment Stations
A.C. True: Director

Prepared by
C.F. LANGWORTHY
Expert in Charge of Nutrition Investigations

It will be noticed that the amount of water varies largely. In the smoked fish, the water having been extracted, the proportion of nutriment is large. It will also be seen that the nutritive value of the oyster is low, although it should be remembered that it is valuable in some cases of weak digestion.

COMPOSITION OF FOOD MATERIALS

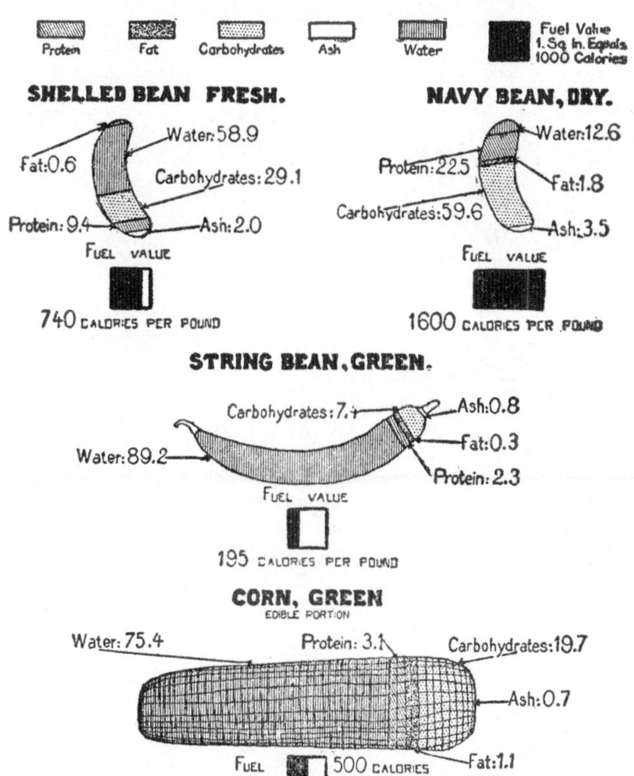

The dry vegetables contain the largest proportion of strength, but the green vegetables give more "tonic" to the blood, and if they are used are a safeguard against certain diseases, such as scurvy.

COMPOSITION OF FOOD MATERIALS

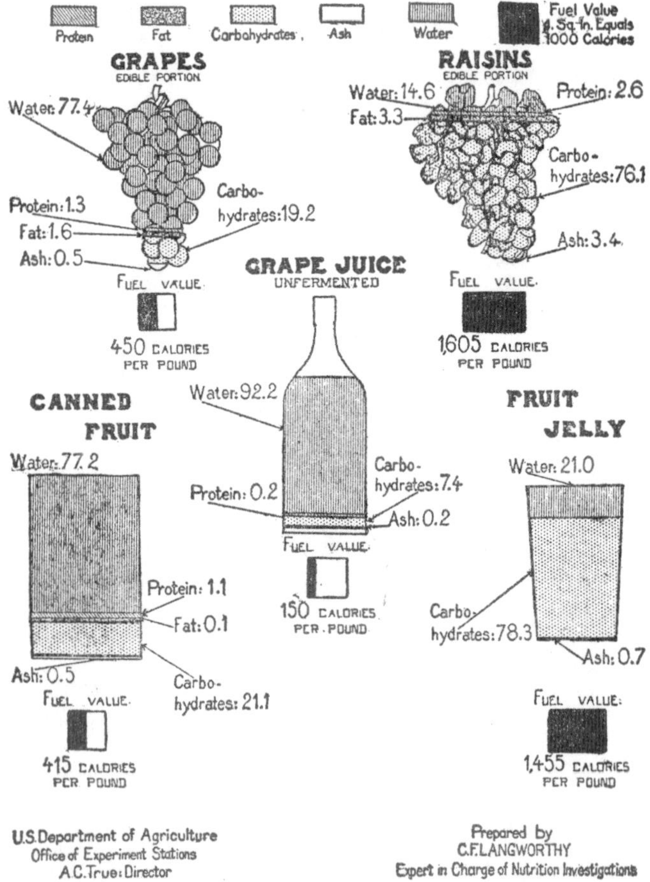

The different fruits are valuable chiefly for the acid and mineral salts they contain, the difference in canned fruit and jelly being the varying amount of water and sugar.

COMPOSITION OF FOOD MATERIALS

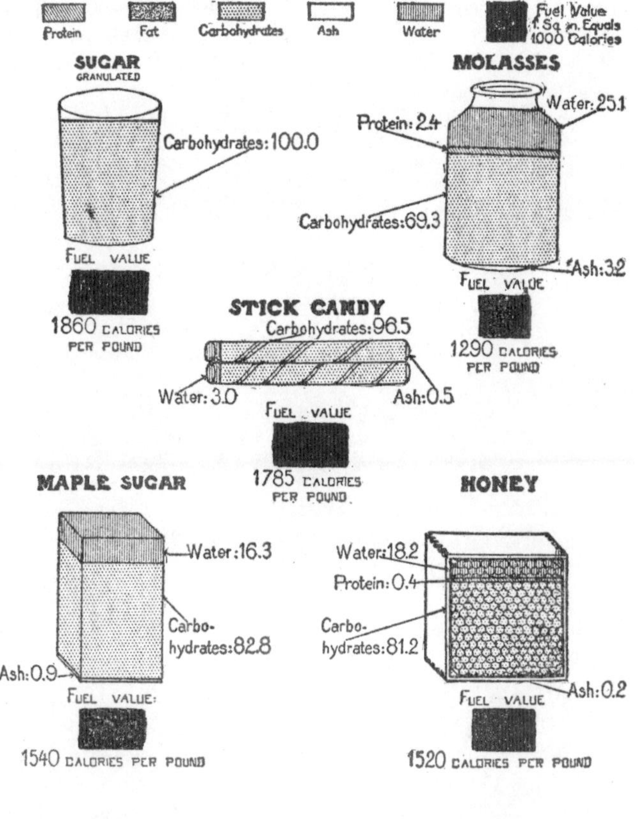

U.S. Department of Agriculture
Office of Experiment Stations
A.C. True: Director

Prepared by
C.F. LANGWORTHY
Expert in Charge of Nutrition Investigations

The careful use of pure sugar and candy is of great help in making a diet well proportioned, although if used to excess sugar will irritate the stomach and bowels. Molasses cakes are valuable for children. This entire group of food gives a great deal of heat to the body.

HOW TO READ THE GAS METER

Read to the right or left as the arrow indicates and take the figures last passed by the hands on the dials.

In the diagram below it would show that the dials registered as follows:

The first dial	60,000 feet.
The second dial	7,000 feet.
The third dial	400 feet.

You therefore began the month or term with

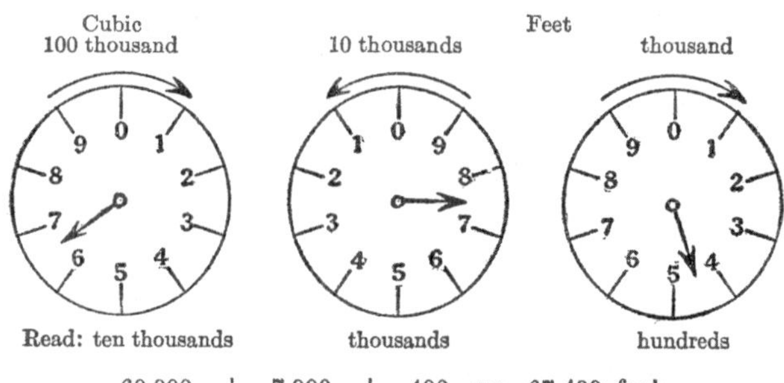

60,000 + 7,000 + 400 = 67,400 feet.

At the end of the month or term, using the same method, it would read,

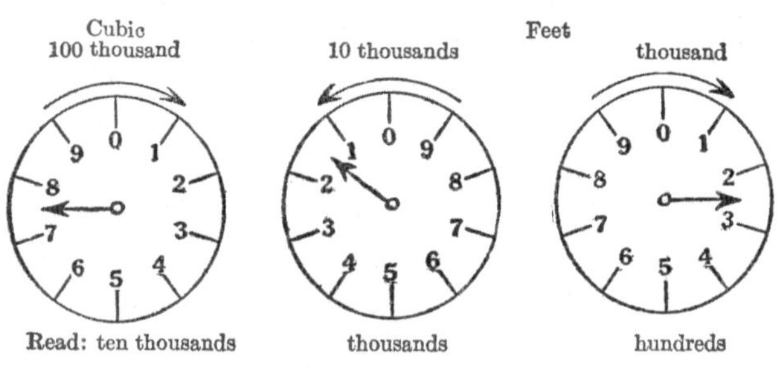

70,000 + 1,000 + 200 = 71,200 feet.

and the difference between the two totals equals the amount (3,800 feet) of gas used.

A COMPARATIVE STUDY OF FUELS FOR THE HOUSEWIFE

The modern housekeeper takes her high calling seriously, and rightly so; she looks carefully to the fuel or food needed to keep the bodily engines of her family in working order; and when this is provided, she turns her attention to the housing of these bodies and the cooking of the aforesaid food.

Fuel for the two latter processes is important, and can be made the basis of very serious study of chemistry, but the purpose of this chapter is to give only a slight working knowledge of the subject, an outline calculated to be of interest, and it is hoped, service, to the average busy housekeeper.

It is well for such a housekeeper to consider the following points in the use of fuels: First, safety; second, economy; third, convenience.

To intelligently decide as to the safety of certain fuels, it is necessary to have at least a slight knowledge of their composition.

In treating the subject, writers, for convenience, usually make the following divisions:

Solid Fuels—coal, wood, coke, charcoal, and peat.
Semi-solid—wax, spermaceti, paraffin.
Liquid—alcohols and oils.
Gaseous—natural and artificial gas.
Electrical—

It should be remembered that the definition of fuel is "a substance producing by its combustion both heat and light."

Fuels are vegetable, animal or mineral in origin, and the amount of heat and light produced varies in proportion. For example, the materials from which candles are made, spermaceti and paraffin, give light but only slight heat, the solid fuels give great heat and only a comparatively dim light, whereas the oils and alcohols give both heat and light.

10

It is not the purpose of this brief chapter to discuss the nature of oxidation and combustion, but rather to concern itself with the practical problems of heating and lighting.

Considered from the standpoint of safety, the solid fuels head the list, while the gases, alcohols and oils need judicious handling, electricity is in a class by itself, and while only a brave person would care to wax eloquent over its origin, modern science does know how to render it comparatively safe as a fuel.

To return to the solid fuels, coal, wood, coke, charcoal and peat, need only to be treated with ordinary common sense, to be quite safe.

The semi-solid fuels, wax, paraffin and spermaceti, belong to the class that furnish light with a negligible amount of heat, so that one needs to preserve only precaution in keeping inflammable materials away from the flame of candles, comprised of these substances.

Coming to the alcohols and oils we need to exercise great care in adapting them to our use.

The two kinds of alcohol used as fuel are ethyl or "ninety-five per cent alcohol" and "wood alcohol." They are of different origin, the former is obtained by fermentation of sugar, the latter by "destructive distillation" of wood. Both kinds of alcohol burn easily, and great care must be exercised to keep them away from flame. This must be specially borne in mind when filling alcohol lamps or stoves.

Wood alcohol has been so treated that it cannot be used for drinking, but its properties as a fuel have not been impaired.

The oils come next in our outline, and we need concern ourselves only with those used as fuels, that is, the mineral oils.

Quite within the memory of many now living whale oil was the one in general use, but at present kerosene has entirely supplanted it.

The more combustible of the mineral oils, that is, the gasoline products, are very unsafe for household use, and should be handled only by experts when used in machinery.

As to kerosene, the time for excessive fear of it is passed, since methods of refining are so improved as to render it a safe fuel for lamps and stoves, provided that ordinary care is exercised.

Gaseous fuels are familiar to most of us, although in some localities not much is known of natural gas, and in fact, the supply is rapidly diminishing where it has been plentiful.

In the case of artificial gas, we have a fuel that serves us well if we look to the piping and fixtures, but care must be taken to detect leaks.

The gases most used in country districts are gasoline gas and acetylene gas, and of the two, the former is far less explosive.

We come now to a brief consideration of the relative cost of fuels. The simplest method will be to estimate roughly the cost per hour of each.

Coal	4	cents an hour.
Gas	3	" " "
Kerosene	.007	" " "
Electricity	8	" " "

Robert Coit Chapin's estimate for a four-room apartment for a year, is as follows:

Coal, three tons, at $6.50	$19.50	
Wood and matches	3.00	
Gas, $2 a month in summer / Gas, $1 a month in winter	18.00	
		$40.50

The estimate is, of course, for an apartment without steam heat, but will serve as a basis for calculation, in determining proportion of income to be spent for the rent of steam-heated rooms.

The question of convenience must be decided by individuals and surroundings, but generally speaking the solid fuels are most useful because of the lack of necessity for special piping. Kerosene and electricity may be regarded largely as adjuncts.

MANAGING A GAS RANGE

General Rules

1. Before lighting the match, make yourself familiar with all the pipes, following each pipe to the burner to which it belongs, so that when a key is turned you will know where to apply the match.

2. To light a top burner, strike the match first, then turn on the gas and apply match instantly.

3. If air gets into the pipe so that the gas burns red, turn off the flow, turn on again to let out the air and finally close the burner and let it remain closed for a moment and it is then ready to light.

4. To light the oven burner, open doors, turn on the pilot light and apply the match; then turn both side keys, and when burners are both lighted shut off the pilot light.

5. Keep all parts of the stove clean.

6. Keep all keys turned tight when not in use.

7. After cooking is begun, lower the gas or use the simmering burner if there is one; a low heat will continue the boiling process after it is once begun.

8. If you have reason to suspect a leak, send for some one at once to attend to it.

GLOSSARY

Agneau. Lamb.
Agra dolce (sour sweet). An Italian sauce.
À la, au aux. With or dressed in a certain style.
Allemande (à la). In German style.
Ambrosia. Food for the gods. Often applied to a fruit salad.
Américaine (à l'). In American style.
Asperges. Asparagus.
Au gratin. With browned crumbs.
Aurora sauce. A white sauce to which lobster butter is added.
Avena. Oats.

Baba Cakes. Cakes baked in small moulds; made from a yeast dough mixture to which is added butter, sugar, eggs, raisins, and almonds. Served as a pudding with hot sauce.
Bain-Marie. A vessel of any kind containing heated water, in which other vessels are placed in order to keep their contents heated.
Bannocks. Scottish cakes made of barley or oatmeal, cooked on a griddle.
Bards. Slices of pork or bacon to lay on the breast of game for cooking.
Basil. A pot herb.
Bay leaves. Leaves from a species of laurel.
Béarnaise (à la). In Swiss style.
Béarnaise sauce. Named from Béarnaise, Swiss home of Henry VIII.
Béchamel (à la). With sauce made of chicken stock and milk or cream.
Biscuit Glacé. Small cakes of ice cream.
Bisque. A soup usually made from shellfish; or an ice cream to which is added finely chopped nuts.
Blanch (to). To whiten.
Blanquette. White meat in cream sauce.
Bœuf braisé. Braised beef.
Bœuf à la jardinière. Braised beef with vegetables.
Bombe glace. Moulded ice cream and ice, or two kinds of ice cream. Outside of one kind, filling of another.
Bouquet of herbs. A sprig each of thyme, savory, marjoram, and parsley.
Bourgeoise (à la). In family style.
Bretonne sauce. A stock sauce in which chopped parsley is served.

Café noir. Black coffee.
Cervelles de veau. Calf's brains.

Chartreuse. A mould of aspic in which there are vegetables; a meat preparation filling the center of the mould. Used to denote anything concealed.
Chateaubriand. A cut from the center of a fillet of beef.
Chaud-froid. Literally hot cold. In cookery a jellied sauce.
Chou-fleur. Cauliflower.
Chutney. An East India sweet pickle.
Civet. A game stew.
Compotes. Fruits stewed in syrup and kept in original shape.
Consommé de volaille. Chicken soup.
Créole (à la). With tomatoes.
Croûte au pot. A brown soup poured over small pieces of toast.
Curry powder. A yellow powder of which the principal ingredient is turmeric. Used largely in India.

De, d'. Of.
Devilled. Highly seasoned.
Dinde farcie. Stuffed turkey.

Écossaise (à l'). In Scottish style.
En coquilles. In shells.
En papillotes. In papers.
Espagnole sauce. A rich brown sauce.

Farci-e. Stuffed.
Fillet de bœuf piqué. Larded fillet of beef.
Foie de veau grillé. Broiled liver.
Fondue. A dish prepared of cheese and eggs.
Fraises. Strawberries.
Frappé. Semi-frozen.
Fricassé de poulet. Fricassée of chicken.
Fromage. Cheese.

Gâteau. Cake.
Gelée. Jelly.
Glacé. Iced or glossed over.
Grilled. Broiled.

Hachis de bœuf. Beef hash.
Hoe cakes. Cakes made of white cornmeal, salt, and boiling water; cooked on a griddle.
Homard. Lobster.
Hors-d'œuvres. Side dishes.
Huîtres en coquille. Oysters in shell.
Huîtres frites. Fried oysters.

Italienne (à l'). In Italian style.

Jardinière. Mixed vegetables.

Kuchen. German for cake.

Lait. Milk.
Laitue. Lettuce.

Macaroni au fromage. Macaroni with cheese.
Macédoine. A mixture of several kinds of vegetables.
Maigre. A vegetable soup without stock.
Maître d'hôtel. Head steward.
Mango. A fruit of the West Indies, Florida, and Mexico.
Mango pickles. Stuffed and pickled young melons and cucumbers.
Maraschino. A cordial.
Marrons. Chestnuts.
Menu. A bill of fare.
Morue. Salt cod.

Noël. Christmas.
Noir. Black.
Nouilles. Noodles.

Œufs farcis. Stuffed eggs.
Œufs pochés. Poached eggs.
Omelette aux fines herbes. Omelette with fine herbs.

Pain. Bread.
Panade. Bread and milk cooked to a paste.
Paté de biftecks. Beefsteak pie.
Paté de foie gras. A paste made of fatted geese livers.
Pois. Peas.
Pommes. Apples.
Pommes de terre. Potatoes.
Pommes de terre à la Lyonnaise. Lyonnaise potatoes.
Pone cakes. A cake made in the South, baked in the oven.
Potage. Soup.
Poulets sautés. Fried chicken.

Queues de bœuf. Ox-tails.

Ragoût. A highly seasoned meat dish.
Réchauffés. Warmed over dishes.
Removes. The roasts or principal dishes.

Salade de laitue. Lettuce salad.
Salade de légumes. Vegetable salad.
Salpicon. Highly seasoned minced meat mixed with a thick sauce.
Sippets. English for croûtons.
Soufflé. Literally, puffed up.
Soupe à l'ognon. Onion soup.
Sucres. Sweets.

Tarte aux pommes. Apple pie.
Tourte. A tart.

WEDDING ANNIVERSARIES

First Year	*Cotton*
Second Year	*Paper*
Third Year	*Leather*
Fifth Year	*Wooden*
Seventh Year	*Woolen*
Tenth Year	*Tin*
Twelfth Year	*Silk and Linen*
Fifteenth Year	*China*
Twenty-fifth Year	*Silver*
Thirtieth Year	*Pearl*
Fortieth Year	*Ruby*
Fiftieth Year	*Golden*
Seventy-fifth Year	*Diamond*

BIRTH MONTH GEMS, FLOWERS, ETC.

January	Garnet	Courtesy	Wildrose
February	Amethyst	Contentment	Pink
March	Bloodstone	Courage	Violet
April	Diamond	Innocence	Easter Lily
May	Emerald	Success in Love	Lily of the Valley
June	Pearl	Purity	Rose
July	Ruby	Nobility of Mind	Daisy
August	Moonstone	Conjugal Felicity	Pond Lily
September	Sapphire	Chastity	Poppy
October	Opal	Hope	Cosmos
November	Topaz	Fidelity	Chrysanthemum
December	Turquoise	Success	Holly

INDEX TO RECIPES

Apple Compote, 76
  Pudding, 95
  Sauce, 76
  Tapioca, 95
Apples, Baked, 76

Bacon, Broiled, 86
Banana Salad, 105
Bananas, 77
  Baked, 77
Batter, 74
Batters, 41
  and Doughs, Table of, 48-49
Beef Cutlets Braised, 84
  Dried, 57
  Hearts En Casserole, 53
  Juice, 115
  Loaf, 84
  Roast, 88
  Scraped, 115
  Tea, 115
Berries, 77
Beverages, Cold, 33
  Fruit, 33
  Hot, 34
Birth Month Gems, Flowers, etc., 152
Biscuits, Baking Powder, 39
  Drop, 40
Bread, Brown, 39
  Making, 37
  Nut, 38, 92
  Oatmeal, 38
  Sticks, 38
  White, 38
Breads, Baking Powder, 39
  Yeast, 38
Brewis, 116
Buckwheat Cakes, 41
Butter, to Cream, 107

Cake, 43
  Baking Powder Sponge, 43
  Black Chocolate, 43
Cake, Harlequin, 44
  Mechanics' Institute, 44
  One Egg Layer, 45
  Soft Molasses, 45
  Spice without Eggs, 45
  White, 46
Cakes, Buckwheat, 41
  Fried, 40
  Graham Drop, 40
  Mashed Potato, 74
  Short, 40
Candy, Maple Sugar, 62
Canning and Preserving, 50
    Suitable Fruits for, 51
Caramel for Flavoring, 62
Caramels, 80
  Chocolate, 61
Carrots and Peas, 117
Casserole Cooking, 52
Catsup, Tomato, 101
Cereal and Cheese, 58
  Gems, 55
  Moulded with Fruit, 54
  Puddings, 55
  with Dates, 55
  with Raisins, 55
Cereals, 54
  Table for, 54
Chafing Dish Cookery, 56
Charlotte Russe, 96
Cheese, 58
  and Cereal, 58
  and Rice with Brown Gravy, 60
  Balls, 60
  Crackers, 60
  Custard, 60
  Fondu, 58
  Grated, 60
  Hominy Baked with, 59
  How to Use, 58
  Porridge, 60
  Toast, 59
Chicken, Broiled, 87
  En Casserole, 52

Chicken, Fried, 87
Roast, 87
Gravy, 87
Salad, 103
Chocolate, 34
Caramels, 61
Ice Cream, 79
Sauce for Ice Cream, 79
Chops, 19
Shoulder En Casserole, 53
to Broil, 83
Veal, 53
Clams and Oysters, Fried, 71
Fried, 70
Steamed, 70
Cocoa, 35
Shells, 35
and Coffee, 36
Codfish, Creamed, 70
Hash, 70
Coffee, After Dinner, 36
Breakfast, 35
Coffees, Cereal, 34, 36
Compote, Apple, 76
Confections, 61
Cookery, Principles of, 29
Cookies, Ginger, 44
Nut, 92
Sugar, 46
Cooking for Invalids, 115
Processes, 32
Cornstarch, Thickening with, 31
Corn Oysters, 117
Pone, 42
Crabs, 71
Cream, Fruit, 79
Creamed Dishes, 56
Croquettes, Meat, 74
Rice, 75
to Shape, 75
Vegetable, 74
Custard, Baked, 95
Frozen, 80
Plain Boiled, 97
Cutlets, Beef, Braised, 84
Veal, 89

Date Whip, 97
Dates, 77
Decorations, 63
Desserts, Frozen, 79
Diet Needs, How Occupation Influences, 16
Dough, Baking Powder, 38
Doughs and Batters, Table of, 48-49
Dressing, French, 103
Lemon, 47
Mayonnaise, 104

Egg and Orange, 116
Creamy or Cuddled, 65
Dishes, 56
How to Tell Age of, 22
Nog, 116
Poached, 66
Timbales, 67
Eggplant, 118
Eggs, 65
Baked, 67
Boiled, 65
Cooking of, 30
Fried, 65
Scrambled, 65
Stuffed, 67

Fats, Cooking of, 30
Finnan Haddie, 73
Fireless Cookers, 24
Home-made, 25
Use of, 25
Fish, 68
Baked, 69
Sauce for, 72
Balls, 71
Boiled, 69
Broiled, 70
Creamed, 71
Planked, 73
Preparation of, for Cooking, 68
Shell, 68
to Select, 68
Flavoring, 30
Caramel for, 62
Flour, Thickening with, 31
Fondant, 61
Food, Care of, 27
Classes of, 14
for Child—One Year to Eighteen Months, 114
Materials, Composition of, 134-143

Food of Infants, 114
  Values, 13
Foods Allowed Child Two to Four Years, 15
    Four to Eight Years, 15
    Eight Years and Upward, 15
  Forbidden All Children, 16
  Starchy, Cooking of, 31
French Dressing, 103
Fritters, 74
Frosting, Apple, 47
  Chocolate, 46
  Chocolate No. 2, 46
  Confectioners', 47
  Cream Caramel, 47
  Plain, Boiled, 46
  Strawberry, 47
Fruit, Cream, 79
  Dessert, 78
  Dried, 77
  for Canning, Selection of, 50
  How to Buy, 20
  Salad, 102
  Toast, 78
Fruits, 76
  Serving of, 76
Frying, 74
Fudge, 61
Fuels for the Housewife, A Comparative Study of, 145

Game, 86
Gas Meter, How to Read, 144
Gas Range, Managing a, 148
Gelatine Dishes, 99
  with Ice Cream, 80
Ginger Bread, Hot Water, 44
    Sour Milk, 45
Glossary, 149
Government Bulletins, 133
Grapefruit, 78
Grape Juice, 34
Gravy, Brown, 86
Groceries, How to Buy Staple, 20

Ham, Boiled, 84
Hash, Codfish, 70
  Corned Beef, 56, 85
Health, General, 16
Heart, Braised, 84
Herring, Kippered, 72
Hominy Baked with Cheese, 59

Ice Cream, Banana, 80
    Caramel, 80
    Chocolate, 79
    Chocolate Sauce for, 79
    for One, 116
    Philadelphia, 79
    with Gelatine, 80
Ices, Water, 79
Italian Pastes, Cooking of, 81

Jars, to Clean, 50
Jelly, Fruit, 99
  Lemon, 99
Jellied Walnuts, 99
Jellies, 51
  Other, 99
Johnny Cake, 42
Junket, Recipe for, 90

Kitchen, The Dangers of the, 27

Lamb En Casserole, 53
  Fricassée of, 86
Lemonade, 33
Liver, Beef's, 84
Lobster, 72
  Creamed, 72
  Salad, 104
Luncheon of Bread and Milk, 18

Macaroni and Cheese, Creamed, 82
  and Other Italian Pastes, 81
  and Oysters, 82
  Baked, with Cheese, 81
  Creamed, 59
  Creole Style, 82
  Scalloped, 82
Macedoine Salad, 104
Marmalade, Orange, 51
Mayonnaise Dressing, 104
Meal, Nut, 92
Meat, Cooking of, 30
  Croquettes, 74
  for Braising, Boiling, and Stewing, 19
  for Pot Roast, Baking, etc., 20
  for Roasting, 20

Meat, How to Buy, 19
How to Cook, 83
Pan Broiled, 86
Table of Cuts of, 19
Meats, Cuts of, 21
Menus, 121-132
Meringue, 97
Milk, 90
Cooking of, 30
How to Buy, 18
Modified, 114
Mince Meat, 94
Minced Meat on Toast, 56
Muffins, Plain, 42
Mush, Fried, 55

Nut Bread, 92
Cookies, 92
Meal, 92
Salad, 92

Omelet, Plain, 66
with Cheese, 57
Omelets, Suggestions to Vary, 66
Onions, Pickled, 100
Scalloped, 118

Orangeade, 34
Oranges, 78
Ox-Tail Soup, 109
Oyster Soup, 109
Stew, 109
Oysters and Clams, Fried, 71
Broiled, 71
Creamed, 73
Scalloped, 73

Pan Cakes, Bread and Rice, 42
Corn Meal, 41
Pastes, Italian, Cooking of, 81
Peanut Taffy, 62
Pear Salad, 104
Peas and Carrots, 117
Peppers, Stuffed, 119
Pickle, End of Season, 100
Pickles, Little, 101
Sweet Cucumber, 101
Pie, Apple, 93
Chocolate, 94
Cottage, 85
Cream, 94
Pie, Custard, 93
Lemon, 93
Pies, 93
Berry, 93
Crust for Two, 93
Pot, 88
Prune, 94
Pumpkin, 94
Rhubarb, 94
Squash, 94
Pigs in Blankets, 73
Pop Overs, 41
Potato, Baked, 118
Salad, 103
Cooked Dressing for, 103
Potatoes, Creamed, 118
Mashed, 118
Poultry, 87
Preserve, Strawberry, 51
Preserving, 51
Prunes, Stewed, 78
Pudding, Apple, 95
Cheese, 59
Chocolate, 96
Chocolate Bread, 96
Cornstarch, 96
Cottage, 96
Fruit, 97
Rice, without Eggs, 98
with Sugar and Cinnamon, 98
Sauce, 97, 98
Simple Puff, 98
Puddings and Sauce, 95

Quinces, 77

Rarebit, 59
Chafing Dish, 57
Relishes, 100
Rhubarb, Stewed, 78
Rice and Cheese with Brown Gravy, 60
Croquettes, 75
Dessert, 98
Rolls, Fruit, 39

Salad, Banana, 105
Chicken, 103
Combination, 105
Fruit, 102
Lobster, 103

Salad, Macedoine, 103
Nut, 92
Pear, 104
Potato, 103
Salmon, 104
Stuffed Tomato, 105
Salad and Dressings, 102
Salmon, Baked Canned, 69
Sandwich, Club, 107
Sandwiches, 106
Meats Good for, 106
Other Attractive, 106
Plain Lettuce, 107
Sauce for Baked Fish, 73
White, 31
Medium, 32
Thick, 32
Thin, 32
Sausages, Savory (Chafing Dish), 88
Scallops, 72
Scalloped Rice and Meat, 88
Shell Fish, 68
Shrimps, 71
Shrub, 34
Soup, Black Bean, 110
Chestnut, 91
Cream of Asparagus, 113
Celery, 112
Corn, 112
Onion, 112
Pea, 112
Potato, 113
Tomato, 113
Hit and Miss, 110
Lentil, 111
Oatmeal, 110
Ox-Tail, 109
Oyster, 109
Parsnip, 110
Pea and Tomato, 110
Potato, 111
Split Pea, 111
Tomato, 111
Vegetable, 111
Soups, 108
Additions, 109
Cream, 112
Soups, Meat, 108
Seasoning, 109
Without Stock or Milk, 110
Special Cooking, 114
Squash, Steamed, 119
Steak, Flank, 85
Hamburg, Broiled, 89
Steaks, 19
to Broil, 83
Stew, Irish, 85
Oyster, 109
with Border of Pink Rice, 98
Stock, Fish, 108
Pot, the, 109
Stuffing, 87

Table, Arranging an Attractive, 2
of Batters and Doughs, 48-49
Taffy, 62
Peanut, 62
Tea, 35
Cambric, for Children, 36
Toast, Cheese, 59
French, 57
Fruit, 78
Tomato Relish, 101
Tomatoes, Fried Green, 118
Tongue, Boiled, 89
Tripe, 88
Reheated, 89
Turkey, Roast, 87
Gravy, 87

Veal, Creamed, 85
Loaf, 89
Vegetable Croquettes, 74
Vegetables, 117
a Quick Way to Cream, 119
Canning of, 50
Cooking of, 31, 117
En Casserole, 53
How to Buy, 20

Waffles, 42
Water, Cold, 33
Ices, 79
Wedding Anniversaries, 152

TABLE OF WEIGHTS AND MEASURES

		equal	
3	teaspoonfuls	equal	1 tablespoonful
16	tablespoonfuls	"	1 cupful
8	ounces	"	1 cupful
16	ounces	"	1 lb.
2	cupfuls	"	1 pint
2	pints	"	1 quart
3 ½	to 4 lbs.	"	1 " (dry)
8	quarts	"	1 peck
4	pecks	"	1 bushel
2	cupfuls butter	"	1 lb.
2	" sugar	"	1 lb.
4	" flour	"	1 lb.
3 ½	cupfuls confectioner's sugar	"	1 lb.
2⅔	cupfuls brown sugar	"	1 lb.
2⅔	" oatmeal	"	1 lb.
2⅔	" cornmeal	"	1 lb.
4 ½	" graham flour	"	1 lb.
4⅓	" coffee	"	1 lb.
8–9	eggs	"	1 lb.

TABLE OF ABBREVIATIONS

Tsp.........teaspoon
Tbsp........tablespoon
Cup.........cup
f.g.........few grains
Spk.........speck
Oz..........ounce

Pt...........pint
Qt...........quart
Pk...........peck
Bu...........bushel
Lb...........pound

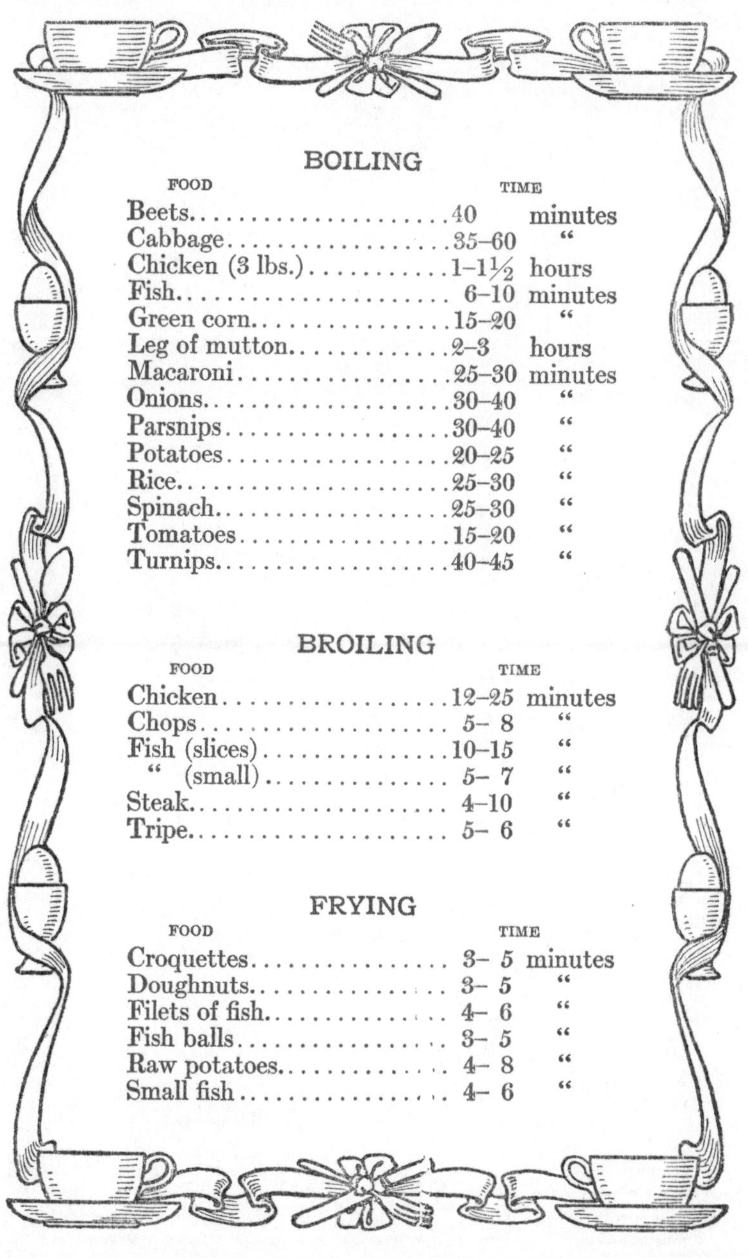

BOILING

FOOD	TIME	
Beets	40	minutes
Cabbage	35–60	"
Chicken (3 lbs.)	1–1½	hours
Fish	6–10	minutes
Green corn	15–20	"
Leg of mutton	2–3	hours
Macaroni	25–30	minutes
Onions	30–40	"
Parsnips	30–40	"
Potatoes	20–25	"
Rice	25–30	"
Spinach	25–30	"
Tomatoes	15–20	"
Turnips	40–45	"

BROILING

FOOD	TIME	
Chicken	12–25	minutes
Chops	5– 8	"
Fish (slices)	10–15	"
" (small)	5– 7	"
Steak	4–10	"
Tripe	5– 6	"

FRYING

FOOD	TIME	
Croquettes	3– 5	minutes
Doughnuts	3– 5	"
Filets of fish	4– 6	"
Fish balls	3– 5	"
Raw potatoes	4– 8	"
Small fish	4– 6	"

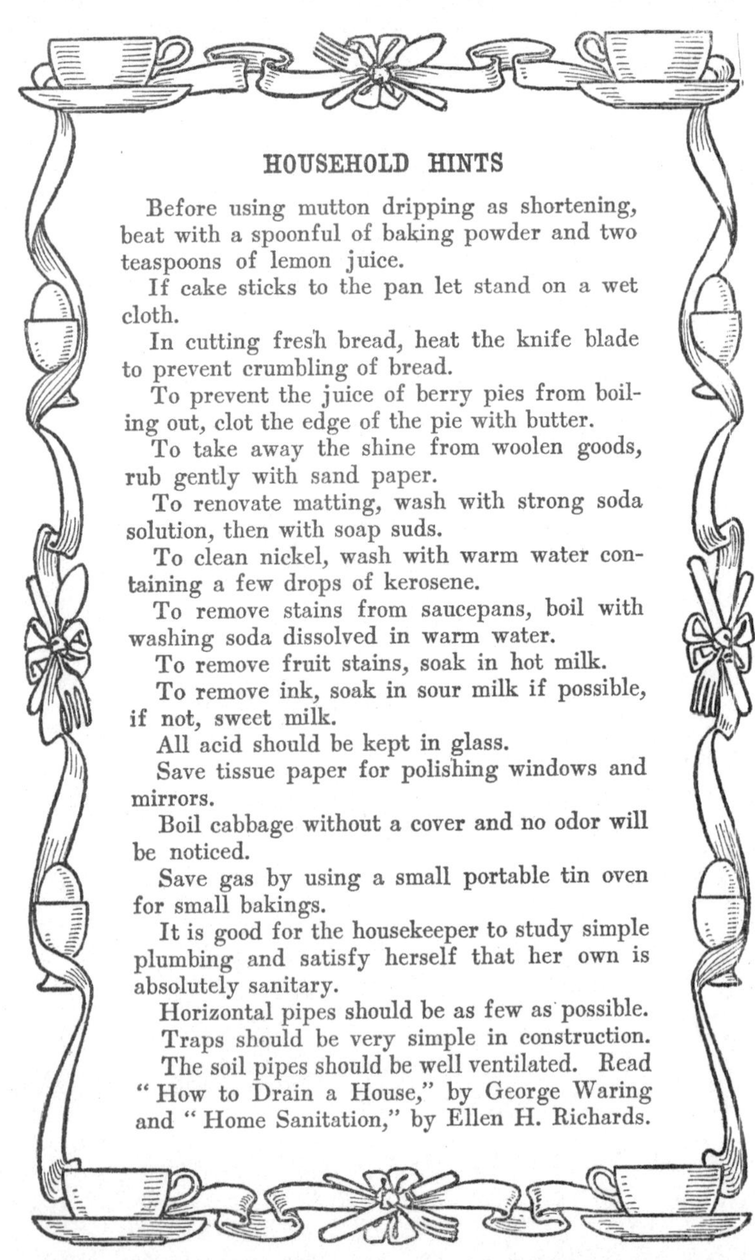

HOUSEHOLD HINTS

Before using mutton dripping as shortening, beat with a spoonful of baking powder and two teaspoons of lemon juice.

If cake sticks to the pan let stand on a wet cloth.

In cutting fresh bread, heat the knife blade to prevent crumbling of bread.

To prevent the juice of berry pies from boiling out, clot the edge of the pie with butter.

To take away the shine from woolen goods, rub gently with sand paper.

To renovate matting, wash with strong soda solution, then with soap suds.

To clean nickel, wash with warm water containing a few drops of kerosene.

To remove stains from saucepans, boil with washing soda dissolved in warm water.

To remove fruit stains, soak in hot milk.

To remove ink, soak in sour milk if possible, if not, sweet milk.

All acid should be kept in glass.

Save tissue paper for polishing windows and mirrors.

Boil cabbage without a cover and no odor will be noticed.

Save gas by using a small portable tin oven for small bakings.

It is good for the housekeeper to study simple plumbing and satisfy herself that her own is absolutely sanitary.

Horizontal pipes should be as few as possible.

Traps should be very simple in construction.

The soil pipes should be well ventilated. Read "How to Drain a House," by George Waring and "Home Sanitation," by Ellen H. Richards.